Professionalization and Activism In Social Work

Professionalization and Activism in Social Work: The Sixties, the Eighties, and the Future

**LINDA CHERREY REESER
AND IRWIN EPSTEIN**

COLUMBIA UNIVERSITY PRESS New York

Earlier versions of parts of chapters 1, 3, and 4 appeared as: Linda Cherrey Reeser, "Specialization, Professionalization, and Social Activism," *Journal of Independent Social Work*, vol. 2, no. 4, Copyright © 1988, Haworth Press, Inc.; an earlier version of chapter 1 appeared as: Linda Cherrey Reeser and Irwin Epstein, "Social Workers' Attitudes Toward Poverty and Social Action: 1968–1984," *Social Service Review*, vol. 61, no. 4, Copyright © 1987, University of Chicago Press; an earlier version of part of chapter 2 appeared as: Linda Cherrey Reeser, "Women and Social Work Activism in the 1980s," *Affilia*, vol. 3, no. 3, Copyright © 1988, Sage Publications, Inc.; an earlier version of part of chapter 4 will appear as: Linda Cherrey Reeser, "Professionalization, Striving, and Social Work Activism," *Journal of Social Service Research*, vol. 13, in late 1989, Copyright © 1989, Haworth Press, Inc.

Columbia University Press
New York   Oxford
Copyright © 1990 Columbia University Press
All rights reserved

Library of Congress Cataloging-in-Publication Data

Reeser, Linda Cherrey.
Professionalization and activism in social work : the sixties, the eighties, and the future / Linda Cherrey Reeser and Irwin Epstein.
p.   cm.
Includes bibliographical references.
ISBN 0-231-06788-7 (alk. paper)
1. Social workers—United States—Attitudes.   2. Social service—United States.   I. Epstein, Irwin.   II. Title.
HV40.8.U6R44   1989   89-17470
361.3'2—dc20   CIP

Casebound editions of Columbia University Press Books are Smyth-sewn and printed on permanent and durable acid-free paper

∞

Printed in the United States of America

10 9 8 7 6 5 4 3 2 1

To those who have continued to struggle
with the issue of social work's responsibility
to the poor and disenfranchised.

CONTENTS

LIST OF TABLES _____

FOREWORD

The emergence of the welfare state in Western Industrial societies reflected the convergence of several broad trends. One was ideological. The welfare state could not develop until people came to define economic rights as political rights. But nineteenth-century *laissez-faire* ideas propagated by the wealthy and privileged inhibited the politicizing of economic relations. The economy was defined as a construct of nature, not a construct of men and women; and it was ostensibly governed by natural laws that would inevitably be disturbed by human interventions. This ideology served economic elites well. On the one side, it provided "scientific" justification for warding off demands by working people for protection from market forces, whether by means of unionization or of state programs. On the other side, it obscured the extent to which state policies in fact aided capital in the struggle with labor. The militia and judiciary could thus be mobilized to break strikes in the name of shielding the natural workings of the market from interference and disruption by labor, without it being evident to many people that state power thereby strengthened employers and weakened workers.

But the fiction of state neutrality in the struggle between capital and labor gradually eroded, in part because it was contradicted by the enlarging role of the state in response to the demands of a rapidly expanding industrial capitalism. The Great Depression especially laid this hypocrisy bare, for it was then that employers were forced more publicly than ever before to call upon government to intervene with a host of measures to restore profits

And it was then that working people could also call upon government to enact programs to protect them as well.

Still, class struggles are not waged with ideas alone. The second coverging trend was mass industrialization which consolidated a vast class of wage workers, thus providing the necessary solidarities to give political weight to the gradually emerging concept of economic rights. The 1930s thus saw the rise of the greatest movements of the unemployed, of industrial workers, and of the elderly in American history, both in the streets and at the polls. In the context of electoral instability and realignment, of protest marches and strike waves, the state was finally forced to concede some economic rights to working people, and to intervene in economic relations to protect those rights. Thus did the state become the main arena within which the continuing struggle between capital and labor was to be played out.

Once inaugurated, welfare state programs empowered working people all the more. On the one hand, the provision of benefits reinforced the ideology of economic rights. On the other, the provision of benefits created new social identities and solidarities by establishing categories of people who received benefits, and who were able to act in concert to defend and expand those benefits. In short, social welfare programs, taken together, brought tens of millions of Americans into new structures and patterns of political relations with the state, thus helping to erode still further the *laissez-faire* prescription that economy and polity be kept strictly separated.

The welfare state also created or expanded a new class of service workers, such as social workers, public health workers, and so forth. In turn, they organized in myriad networks—civil service organizations and unions, professional membership organizations, and associations of agencies. These identities and solidarities also represented new structures and patterns of political relations with the state.

In this insightful and illuminating book, Linda Cherrey Reeser and Irwin Epstein direct our attention to the transforming consequences of these continuing and momentous developments on the occupation of social work. The first of the two sample surveys of professional attitudes and activism of social workers which constitute the data base of this quantitative historical study was conducted in the 1960s, another time of electoral instability and realignment, of protest and marches (in which more than a few social workers were themselves implicated), and of consequent expansion of social and economic entitlements. The second survey was conducted in the 1980s, a time when the resurgent business classes in the United States (and in some other Western industrial countries, notably England) were mobilizing to reassert the primacy of *laissez-faire* ideology over the relations of state and economy, with all that meant for the potential weakening of the ideology of economic rights and the curbing of the social programs, which had given rise to recipient organizations, social service staff organizations, and thus to new sources of political power. Systematic comparison of the two survey samples yields several provocative findings.

One finding is particularly striking: Despite the reassertion of a kind of rugged individualistic ideology in the present period, social workers have resisted it. Far more social workers today think that problems such as poverty are rooted in structural sources than thought so in the 1960s, when essentially individualistic explanations were more in vogue. This shift in explanatory mode is a genuine legacy of the protest movements of the 1960s.

What makes this book all the more interesting and relevant is the bearing of these two surveys, separated as they were by nearly two decades, on the evolution of social work both as profession and as social movement. No other profession exhibits this tension with the same intensity. And that is owed to the fact that the flowing and ebbing of social welfare innovations and expenditures parallels the eruption and subsiding of mass unrest and struggles in the larger society. Nor can the tension be resolved. Like it or not, our fate, and the fate of the programs and agencies in which we find our livelihoods and act on our conflicted moral vision, is ineluctably caught up in larger currents of conflict and contention. We can weigh profession and movement differently, or vary the weight from one time to another, but we cannot escape the dilemma of identity. That, or so it seems to me, is the central message of this fascinating exploration of social worker attitudes toward professionalization and activism. Tensions aside, it is this dualism of purpose that sets us off from most other professions, and gives our work its relatively distinctive moral meaning.

Do research measures suggest that we are becoming more professionalized? So it would seem, though we are far from satisfying traditional criteria. Do correlative research measures show that we are becoming less activist as a result of our greater professionalization? Apparently not. Indeed, it appears that social work involvement in conventional political processes—testifying, lobbying, electoral campaigns, etc.—is greater in the 1980s than it was in the 1960s. To be sure, we are less involved in protest activities, but there is no basis in the data for supposing that support for protest will not re-emerge if a new period of mass unrest and insurgency breaks out in the society. As we professionalize, in short, there is an apparent enlargement of conventional political involvements, punctuated by brief periods of protest involvement. And so the profession/movement tension persists, even as we change.

These findings regarding the continuing or perhaps expanded political activism of social workers, even if the political means employed are relatively conventional, may help explain part of the successful resistance in American society to the corporate/Republican effort to slash and even dismantle social programs during the Reagan years. To be sure, the assault was partly successful; some programs were eliminated and others slashed. But the cuts were far less than the Reagan Administration had initially projected. The public itself was the most important source of resistance: opinion polls show that people believe in social program rights and expect the state to enforce them. Resistance by organized recipient groups, such as the elderly, was also a powerful constraint. And, as these comparative surveys suggest, intensive lobbying by multiple networks of human service workers was also doubtless an important source of political resistance.

And so the message of this unique empirical historical study is heartening. Let us praise the messengers.

Richard A. Cloward
Professor, Columbia
University School of
Social Work

ACKNOWLEDGMENTS _____

Linda Cherrey Reeser worked on the book while teaching and being the Director of Field Education at the School of Social Work at Western Michigan University. She expresses her appreciation to students, faculty, and Dr. Phil Kramer, the Director of the School, for the support they provided.

Her parents, Morris and Lillian Cherrey, gave her the quest for learning, self-discipline, and the love she needed to achieve this goal.

Her husband, Barry, has provided her with the love and moral support to complete this book.

Irwin Epstein's research was conducted under the auspices of the Columbia University School of Social Work's Evaluation Project on Mobilization for Youth, endorsed by NASW's Commission on Social Policy and Action, and funded by the National Institute of Mental Health (MH 01178–01). He wishes to acknowledge Richard A. Cloward, who inspired the original study, and the staff of the Research Department of the Boysville Institute, Boysville of Michigan, who contributed to the completion of the current work.

Sue Timmer helped to complete the many versions of our manuscript. She is much appreciated for her competence, patience, and encouragement.

Professionalization and Activism
In Social Work

INTRODUCTION ⎯⎯⎯⎯⎯⎯⎯⎯⎯⎯⎯⎯⎯⎯⎯⎯⎯⎯⎯⎯

Throughout the history of social work, students, teachers, and practitioners alike have been concerned with the proper role of social work in society. This issue was first articulated in the "cause" versus "function" debate described by Porter Lee (1929). Implicit in this debate are a set of value conflicts that are at the core of the past, present, and future of social work. These conflicts concern whether social work should be primarily a movement designed to bring about social justice and social change or, instead, primarily a profession, with a scientific knowledge base and set of ameliorative skills designed to promote social adjustment. There is concern whether social work's striving to become more professionalized means abandoning social action.

Closely related to the above concerns are questions of whether social work should direct its resources and services to the problems of the poor and the disenfranchised, to all social class groupings and political constituencies, or only to those groups that might benefit most from the skills and knowledge base developed by social work.

These core concerns have been raised in one form or another in "whence and whither" articles and books at critical junctures over the course of social work history (see, for example, Lee 1929; Bisno 1956; Eaton 1956; Benthrup 1964; Toren 1972; Richan and Mendelsohn 1973; Grønbjerg, Street, and Suttles 1978). However, these publications have rarely, if ever, presented empirical data based on the actual professional and political attitudes and behaviors of rank-and-file social workers. Instead, they are generally rhetorical, devoid of empirical data, written by academics, and solely derived from the perceptions and value commitments of their authors.

To this day, the debate continues over whether social work is, or should be, a profession and whether it has abandoned its social action commitments to the poor and oppressed (Bisno 1956; Toren 1972; Dean 1977; Soufleé 1977; Miller 1981; Austin 1985). Elsewhere the conflict is couched in terms of whether social work is a "consenting" or "dissenting" profession (Cooper 1977; Soufle 1977). The former implies accommodation to the status quo; the latter suggests involvement in social change. Irrespective of how the questions are put, the ways in which these fundamental value conflicts are resolved or reconciled will significantly effect the future of social work.

THE SIXTIES VERSUS THE EIGHTIES

Probably no period in history is more reflective of the opposing positions in this debate than that of the sixties and the eighties. The sixties was, of course, a period of widespread social activism exemplified by the War on Poverty and, some would say, anti-professionalism (Haug 1975; Illich 1976). During this period, social activism and professionalization often were viewed as antithetical to each other (Specht 1972).

Since then, social workers and their professional association, the National Association of Social Workers (NASW), have invested considerable resources in the quest for professional status while at the same time they continued their support of social action (Alexander 1982; Minahan 1981; *NASW News* October 1985). The pairing of these two sets of efforts assumes that the two are neither mutually exclusive nor in conflict with each other.

Finally, in contrast with the sixties, the sociopolitical climate of the eighties was much more conservative. With massive cutbacks in social programs, many practicing social workers and social work students aspired to careers in private psychotherapeutic practice and jobs in the corporate sector rather than to government-sponsored programs serving the poor (Chess, Norlin, and Jayaratne 1983; Rubin, Johnson, and DeWeaver 1986; *NASW News*, May 1986).

Conventional wisdom would suggest that, as compared with those of the sixties, social workers in the eighties were more professionalized, less activist, less concerned with the alleviation of poverty and political oppression, and so on. Alternatively, one might argue that since the majority of social workers are female, the greater strength of the women's liberation movement throughout the seventies and eighties might be a basis for greater activism on the part of social workers.

To date, however, there are no empirical studies describing social worker's levels of activism and professionalization in the sixties and eighties. Instead, there is only speculation and concern. Nor are there studies of the relationships between gender, race, age, religion, and other social factors on activism. Finally, there are no studies exploring the relationships between professionalization and social worker activism during these two periods.

PURPOSE OF THE BOOK

This book considers these important questions by comparing the findings of two large, public opinion surveys of rank-and-file social workers conducted in 1968 and 1984. Its purpose is to determine the changes, if any, that may have occurred in the social activism and professionalization of social workers during that space of time. In addition, the book looks at the social action effects of the background characteristics that social workers brought to their work in those two time periods. Finally, the correlations between professionalization and social worker activism in the sixties and eighties are explored. Based on the foregoing statistical analyses, the authors speculate about the "political mythology" of social work and the professional and social-action profiles of future social workers.

THE AUTHORS' APPROACH

Not unlike the "whence and whither" writers of the past, the authors of this book are both academics. In contrast to their predecessors, however, they share a belief that these issues are most effectively discussed and understood through analysis of empirical data drawn from anonymous, self-administered surveys of rank-and- file social workers. Research findings are not immune to differences in interpretation. In an effort to minimize these differences, the authors of this book attempt to write as "close to the data" as possible. This implies a very careful and precise use of language in describing findings. Interpretations and possible explanations are likely to be more free-wheeling.

Another way in which our mutual desire to use language precisely is expressed is in our not referring to social work as a "profession." Although this is somewhat awkward and inconsistent with common parlance (or at least social workers' parlance), it reflects the debate over whether social work constitutes a "full" or merely an "aspiring" profession. In addition, it reflects differences in the sociological interpretation of existing empirical data concerning this issue (Epstein and Conrad 1978). Perhaps this is a half empty/half full question. Nevertheless, by referring to social work as an "occupation" or as a "field" rather than as a "profession," this unresolved empirical and ideological question is highlighted.

A final semantic note involves our effort to avoid using the oftentimes misleading and ambiguous terms "conservative" or "radical" to describe social workers' lesser or greater activism. In common usage, these terms often, but not always confound two dimensions. The first refers to the extremity of social or political action that is contemplated or engaged in. The second involves issues related to political ideology, i.e., the political right versus left dimension. The result of this inconsistent usage is confusion and lack of clarity.

Consequently, in the interest of more effective communication and more accurate dissemination of our findings, we use the generic term "activism" to refer to the extent of social or political involvement. References to substantive political attitudes or beliefs use the terms of "conservative," "liberal," or "radical" to describe an ideological continuum from the politically right to the politically left.

Our efforts to communicate our findings clearly and precisely require meticulous writing and careful reading. On that score, we can empathize with the reader. Nonetheless, we ask the reader to be equally careful in citing the results of this unique and potentially controversial study. These are complex and important issues. They deserve to be treated with scholarly care and precision rather than being couched in political or careerist rhetoric.

METHODOLOGY

Study Samples

This book is based on a comparison of two large, public-opinion surveys of rank-and-file members of NASW conducted in 1968 and 1984. The latter survey by Reeser (1986) is a national replication of a New York City survey of NASW members conducted by Epstein (1969) seventeen years earlier. Epstein systematically surveyed every third member of the New York City chapter of NASW. Also employing a systematic sampling method, Reeser surveyed every seventieth member from NASW's national mailing list. Sample sizes are 1020 and 682, respectively. The return rate in Epstein's sample was 65 percent and in Reeser's 57 percent.

Epstein tested the representativeness of his sample by making comparisons between respondents and nonrespondents on such characteristics as agency auspice, agency position, and field of service. No significant differences were found between respondents and nonrespondents or between respondents and national NASW member characteristics. Following similar procedures, Reeser found respondents and nonrespondents to be quite similar on organizational variables.

Comparisons between the 1968 and 1984 samples were made on agency position, field of service, agency auspice, gender, race, and religion. Although the samples were significantly different on all characteristics except gender, these differences do not invalidate comparison of the two samples. Instead they are likely to reflect changes that have occurred in social work since 1968. For example, in comparison with the 1968 sample, a greater proportion of social workers in the 1984 survey were employed in the field of mental health and were in private practice or doing casework in agencies while a lesser proportion were employed in community action agencies and settlement houses and doing community organization.

Moreover, with samples as large as these, very small percentage differences constitute statistically significant differences. In this context, statistically significant differences do not invalidate comparisons between the two samples. If anything, they imply socially significant changes in the characteristics and work commitments of social workers.

Approaches to Data Analysis and Comparisons

In exploring issues related to professionalization and social worker activism in the sixties and in the eighties, several types of data analyses and data comparisons are employed in this book:

(1). *Descriptive analysis within each cohort based on percentage differences.* This might answer such questions as: "What percentage of social workers in 1968 approved the use of protest? and "How does this compare with the percentage of social workers in 1968 approving the use of public testimony?"

(2). *Percentage comparisons between the cohorts*. This might answer such questions as "What percentage of social workers in 1968 approved the use of protest as compared with social workers in 1984?"

(3). *Cross-tabulations within cohorts based on percentage differences*. This might answer the question, "What percentage of caseworkers, group workers, and community organizers approved the use of protest in 1968?"

(4). *Comparisons of cross-tabulations between cohorts*. This might answer the question, "What percentage of caseworkers in 1968 approved the use of protest as compared with caseworkers in 1984?"

(5). *Correlational analysis within cohorts*. This might answer the question, "What was the correlation between social workers' participation in professional activities and approval of protest in 1968?"

(6). *Comparisons of correlations between cohorts*. This might answer the question, "Has the correlation between professional participation and approval of protest changed from 1968 to 1984?"

Although our data analysis is extensive and painstaking, we hasten to assure readers who are research phobic that the research strategy itself is not terribly complicated. Nevertheless, patient and careful reading is required to understand the arguments and evidence presented. The issues that we are researching are, however, quite complex.

By and large, Chi-Square and statistical significance at the .05 level are used to indicate historically as well as statistically significant differences in the two time periods. Occasionally, the more sensitive Wilcoxon measure is used with the Reeser data to explore relationships.

For those who are daunted by the prospect of a correlational analysis, this appears in our last data chapter, but only after a painless reintroduction to correlations and their interpretation. Alternatively, for research mavens desirous of more sophisticated data-analytic approaches we refer you to Reeser (1986) for a discussion of multiple regression analysis based on the 1984 sample.

We have controlled for the effects of years of experience in social work, auspice, position held, and social work training on the relationships between professionalization and activism and demographics and activism. By and large, these variables did not change the relationships. Thus, we only discuss these findings when they lend insight. For example, in chapter 2 they help to explain the relationship between gender and activism.

Our intention in this book is to explore, through survey research methods, a set of questions which have been of concern to social work theoreticians as well as to rank-and-file social workers throughout the history of social work.

Although great quantities of theory and rhetoric have been generated about them, they have rarely been addressed empirically. Our purpose is to pose these important questions, in an answerable fashion, and to answer them, with the attention they deserve, in a manner that is accessible to researchers and nonresearchers alike. This is a tall order, but we feel well worth the effort.

Other Methodological Issues

Since the original data from Epstein's sample are no longer available, some analytic comparisons with Reeser's data are no longer possible. Moreover, Reeser has data concerning relatively recent occupational developments, such as licensure and private practice, that were not tapped in the original survey.

In considering descriptive differences for the 1968 and 1984 samples, identical items are employed. However, in the construction of some indices, slightly different component items were used with the 1968 and 1984 samples. This was because respective factor analyses indicated that a few different questionnaire items had slightly different meanings to respondents at the different points in time. In these few instances we opted for using the different component items in measuring key concepts so as to be true to the contemporaneous samples rather than rigidly employing the same component items across samples.

INTENDED AUDIENCE

This book is written for social work students, practitioners, and educators who are interested in the past, present, and future of social work as a social and political institution. From our perspective, that means every social worker and everyone thinking of becoming a social worker. In addition, t should interest sociologists of occupations and professions as well as politcal scientists concerned with the political impact of occupations on our society.

Despite the foregoing methodological discussion, the book is not written for researchers. And while the reader may encounter some dry spots here and there, we have attempted to write with as little research jargon as is possible without sacrificing precision. Technical writers know how difficult that objective is to achieve. Only the reader can judge how successful we've been. The social and political significance of these issues for today's social workers and for future social workers demand that we try.

ORGANIZATION OF THE BOOK

The data analysis in this book is organized in four chapters. Chapter 1 offers a comparison of social workers' attitudes toward poverty and activism in the sixties and in the eighties. Here, distinctions are made between activist strategies and goals for social work and between different forms of activist behaviors for the occupation as a whole and for practice groups within social work.

In chapter 2, the impact of background factors on activism is discussed. Here we explore the relations between gender, age, race, religion, and political party affiliation on the one hand and activism on the other.

In chapter 3, the relative degree of professionalization of sixties and eighties social workers is described. Here we look at professionalization of the work setting, participation in the occupational community, identification with a reference group, perception of autonomy, and commitment to an ideology of professionalism, for the occupation as a whole and for practice groups within social work.

In chapter 4, the last data chapter, the relative impact of professionalization on activism during the sixties and the eighties is assessed.

In our final chapter, chapter 5, we discuss the implications of our findings for the future of social work. In that chapter, we speculate about why social work's beliefs about its professionalization and activism have persisted historically despite evidence to the contrary. The authors also consider different possible scenarios for future professionalization within social work and present a social action profile of future social workers

There are two appendices to this book. Appendix A discusses ideas for future research on professionalization and activism. Appendix B presents Epstein and Reeser's professionalization and social activism indices.

1

Social Action Attitudes and Behaviors: The Sixties Versus the Eighties

Whether in quest of increased professionalization or social reform, leaders in social work have always exhorted the rank-and-file to become more involved in social action. Social action advocates have differed however about whether social change strategies should be based on professional expertise or direct action (Thursz 1966; MacRae 1966); whether these actions should be taken on behalf of the poor or all social classes (Cloward and Epstein 1965; Stewart 1981); and whether social work intervention strategies and services should be directed toward client adaptation to the existing environment or social and political change (Bisno 1956; Dean 1977; Miller 1981).

As we indicated in the introduction, these debates were rarely informed by empirical research. Consequently, little is known about where most social workers stood in the past and where they stand today on these issues.

This chapter compares social workers' attitudes in the sixties and in the eighties toward poverty, working with low-income clients, and social action goals and strategies. In addition, it considers the actual social action behaviors that respondents engaged in during these two decades. In general, it attempts to answer the question—where did rank-and-file social workers in the two periods stand in regard to poverty, the poor and social action in their behalf? More specifically, it addresses the following questions:

(1). Did social workers in the sixties differ from those in the eighties in their acceptance of individualistic versus structural explanations of poverty?

(2). Has the social class of those receiving social work services changed and have social worker preferences with regard to the social class of their clients changed?

(3). Has there been a reduction in social workers' commitments to activist goals for social work since the sixties?

(4). Were social workers in the sixties more likely to endorse consensus or conflict strategies of social change than their eighties compeers?

(5). Are present-day social workers less activist in their behaviors than their sixties predecessors?

(6). How did practice specialization, i.e., being a caseworker, group worker, community organizer, or private practitioner affect social workers' activism during these historic periods?

NATIONAL SURVEYS OF ATTITUDES TOWARD POVERTY

Before answering the above questions we should point out that a few national surveys were conducted in the sixties and early seventies that provide a profile of popular beliefs during that period about poverty and welfare (Alston and Dean 1972; Feagin 1975). These studies do not report findings by occupation. As a result, for that time period, it is possible only to determine beliefs of middle class professionals in general, but not those of social workers in particular.

In 1985, a national survey conducted by Hendrickson and Axelson did investigate attitudes of computer scientists, public defenders, and social workers toward poverty, the work ethic, and welfare. However, that study is severely limited by the sample's small size. And while Hendrickson and Axelson did draw tentative conclusions about changes in the attitudes of professionals toward the poor, they did so by comparing their results with earlier studies that used questions that were different from theirs. Consequently, their conclusions must be treated as highly speculative.

ATTITUDES TOWARD POVERTY

In an attempt to measure social workers' conceptions of the causes of poverty in the sixties and eighties, respondents were asked to indicate from a range of choices the "two most important reasons for the existence of poverty in the U.S." Response alternatives provided were explanations commonly found in popular and professional discussions about poverty.

One choice can be categorized as an individualistic explanation, which places the blame for poverty on the poor themselves. The response choice was: "poor people are not adequately motivated to take advantage of existing opportunities." Another explanation for poverty, a social structural one, places blame on social and economic conditions; it was represented in the following items: "powerful interests are fundamentally opposed to the solution of the problem of poverty" and "those people who are better off will never give up anything unless forced." The statement "we do not possess the necessary knowledge and techniques" represented a technological explanation for poverty. Finally, interest-group explanations were provided which indicated that groups must compete and negotiate with one another for resources and power to eliminate poverty. These were: "people representing different interests do not often enough sit down together to work out the problem" and "poor people have not been organized to demand better treatment by society."

Conventional wisdom, which asserts that the social workers of the sixties were more "radical" and those of the eighties more "conservative," would suggest that the latter would be more likely to espouse individual explanations and less likely to espouse structural explanations than the former. In other words, social workers of the sixties would be more likely to blame the social stratification system that maintains the gap between rich and poor and those in the eighties more likely to blame the poor themselves.

Table 1.1 shows social workers' responses to this question about the reasons for poverty in 1968 and in 1984. The differences between the two samples were statistically significant, but in a direction quite opposite that which conventional wisdom had predicted. Thus, for example, a greater proportion of respondents in 1984 chose social structural reasons for the existence of poverty than did those in 1968. In 1984, 53 percent of social workers indicated that a primary reason for poverty is that powerful inter-

TABLE 1.1. Opinions in 1968 and 1984 about the Reasons for Poverty

Reason	1968	1984
Individualistic		
Poor Lack Motivation	26%	10%
Social Structural		
Power Interests Opposed	40	53
Upper Class Must Be Forced	12	25
Technological		
Lack Knowledge and Techniques	29	18
Interest Group		
Groups Do Not Work Out the Problem	41	29
Poor Must Organize	45	24

a. All percentage differences are significant by X^2 ($p < .001$).
b. Ns range from 980 to 989 in 1968 and from 671 to 678 in 1984.

ests are opposed to eradicating poverty as compared with 40 percent in 1968. In 1984, 25 percent agreed that force is necessary to get the middle and upper classes to redistribute resources while only 12 percent agreed in 1968. Alternatively, a greater proportion of respondents in 1968 than in 1984 chose an individualistic explanation for the existence of poverty (26% versus 10%) and believed that poverty was the result of lack of knowledge and techniques (29% versus 18%). Further, in 1986, more social workers espoused an interest-group explanation.

Two other items in our surveys tapped attitudes toward poverty. On a Likert-type scale, social workers were asked whether they agreed or disagreed with the following statements: "The only way to do away with poverty is to make basic changes in our political and economic system," and "The poor are in the best position to decide what services they need."

Table 1.2 indicates the percentages in 1968 and 1984 agreeing with these statements about poverty and the poor. The differences between the samples were statistically significant and although contrary to popular belief, consistent with our previous findings. Thus, respondents in 1984 were again more likely than those in 1968 to agree with a social structural explanation of poverty that basic changes must be made in the political and economic system (81% versus 61%) and more likely to believe in self-determination for the poor (51% versus 35%).

Notwithstanding armchair opinion about the greater conservatism of the eighties as compared with the sixties, the discovery that social workers in 1968 were more likely than those in 1984 to attribute poverty to lack of effort on the part of the poor is supported by other public opinion research. Alston and Dean (1972), using data collected by Gallup and Associates, in 1964 found that 34 percent of middle-class professionals placed the blame for poverty on the poor and favored restrictive requirements for welfare assistance. Feagin (1975) reported in a national survey on poverty in 1969 that 50 percent of the middle-income respondents endorsed individualistic explanations for poverty. By contrast, in 1985 Hendrickson and Axelson found in their national survey of the membership of three professional organizations that only 15.9 percent of the respondents attributed poverty to characteristics of the poor, whereas 55.9 percent attributed the causes of poverty to the economic system.

One possible explanation for the apparent change in perceptions about the reasons for poverty over the last two decades is that the middle class has become more sensitized to structural inequities in the socioeconomic system. In the 1960s, in the context of a "War on Poverty," it may have been easier to attribute poverty to the poor not taking advantage of opportunities to help themselves. Moreover, the focus of most of the programs was on rehabilitating the poor. In 1984, a time of high unemployment, media reports of middle-class people losing their jobs through no fault of their own, and major cuts in social programs, it was hard not to be aware of the systemic causes of poverty.

Social workers in 1984 were less likely to believe that more professional knowledge and techniques are needed to eliminate poverty, but more likely to believe that the poor know best what they need. It may be that social workers have become skeptical over time because the application of social work expertise has not solved the problem of poverty.

TABLE 1.2. Percentage in 1968 and 1984 Agreeing with Each Belief About Poverty

Beliefs	1968	1984
Make Basic Changes in System	61%	81%
Poor Decide What They Need	35	51

a. All percentage differences are significant by X^2 ($p < .001$).
b. Ns range from 1010 to 1020 in 1968 and from 675 to 680 in 1984.

Finally, it may be that social workers in the eighties were less likely to accept the pluralistic political perspective that poverty will be eliminated if the poor organize into interest groups and negotiate for resources. Given the Reagan Administration's failure to acknowledge that elimination of poverty should be a high priority item on the national agenda this pessimism is understandable.

CLIENTS' SOCIAL CLASS

In an effort to assess the social class character of social work service recipients in the sixties and the eighties, respondents in both surveys were asked to indicate the social class category that "best describes the clientele" in their agency and were given the following choices: "predominantly middle class," "predominantly lower class," or "about equal representation of all social classes." Next, using these same client categories, respondents were asked to indicate the group with which they "prefer" to work. Table 1.3 describes the social class of respondents' clientele and the preferred social class of clients in 1968 and 1984. Differences between the samples on both dimensions were statistically significant. Thus, although roughly equal proportions of respondents in both periods served exclusively middle-class clients (23% in 1968 versus 27% in 1984), more social workers in 1968 served lower-class clients (50% in 1968 and 42% in 1984) and a greater proportion of social workers in 1984 served an equal distribution of all social classes (32% in 1984 versus 18% in 1968).

TABLE 1.3. Social Class of Actual and Preferred Agency Clients in 1968 and 1984

Social Class	Agency Clients 1968	Preferred Clients 1968	Agency Clients 1984	Preferred Clients 1984
Middle Class	23%	9%	27%	19%
Lower Class	50	23	42	14
All Classes	18	50	32	68

a. All percentage differences are significant by X^2 ($p < .001$).
b. Ns range from 857 to 928 in 1968 and from 640 to 668 in 1984.

When queried about their preferences, the majority of respondents in both periods preferred an equal representation of all income groups as their client preference (68% in 1984 versus 50% in 1968). In both periods as well, a minority of respondents preferred predominantly lower or middle-class clients. However, a greater proportion of social workers in 1968 preferred predominantly lower-class clients (23% in 1968 versus 14% in 1984) and a greater proportion of social workers in 1984 preferred middle-class clientele (19% in 1984 versus 9% in 1968).

These findings suggest that social workers in the sixties were more likely to serve predominantly low income clients and more likely to prefer to do so than their colleagues in the eighties. The expressed preference for serving all social class groups may be a response to the increasing demands of the middle-class for social services. It may also indicate a more socially acceptable way of expressing a preference for working with middle-class clients. Perhaps social workers prefer working with middle class clients who are like themselves and hold similar values. In addition, the technologies social workers employ may be more compatible with the more psychological and less material problem-definitions carried by middle-class clients (Cloward and Epstein 1965). Finally, social workers may be more successful with middle-class clients. By contrast, the problems of the poor (e.g., poverty, delinquency, drug abuse) have proved to be more resistant to the individual and programmatic efforts of the profession and of the society as a whole.

The decline in commitment to serving the poor is also reflected in the greater emphasis on clinical practice in the private sector and the fewer social workers employed in the public sector serving primarily low-income clients. Thus, in the 1968 study, 5 percent of the respondents worked in public assistance compared with 2 percent in the 1984 study. In response to this decline, a recent conference addressed the problems of recruitment and retention of professionally trained social workers in public child welfare services (*NASW News,* May 1986).

Finally, social workers in the 1980s may be more inclined to prefer serving all social classes rather than the poor because claims to professional status and greater public acceptance can be made through association with higher status clients (Cloward and Epstein 1965). Along these lines, Walsh and Elling (1972) demonstrated that members of occupational groups who were actively striving to gain higher status were more negative in their orientation toward lower-income clients than were members of occupations who were less active.

COMMITMENT TO ACTIVIST GOALS

Leaving the issue of preferred social class of clientele, we next considered social workers' preferred goals for their occupational group. One can infer the content of activist goals for social work by looking at conflicts in priorities confronting the field historically. Such conflicts are presented in two comment pieces written in a 1981 issue of *Social Work*. In the first, the author expressed concern over the apparent priority given to psychotherapy at the expense of social reform (Miller). In the second piece, the author decried the "abandonment of the poor" by the social workers (Stewart). There followed a lively debate on the positions expressed by these two social workers (see *Social Work*, "Points and Viewpoints").

Drawing on earlier literature but consistent with this debate, Epstein (1969) developed a "typology" of activist goals. He classified as the least activist those social workers who favor the professional goal of helping individuals of all social classes adjust to the environment. Those social workers committed to societal change on behalf of the poor were assumed to hold the most activist goal orientation. To measure commitment to activist goals, respondents in both surveys were asked to choose between the goals of individual adaptation versus societal change and indicate whether "social work should devote most of its attention and resources" to the poor or to all social classes equally.

Table 1.4 shows the percentage of respondents in 1968 and 1984 who approved each of these activist goals and who approved both of these goals for social work. The findings show that over one-half the respondents in

TABLE 1.4. Percentage in 1968 and 1984 Approving Each Professional Goal

GOAL	1968	1984
Societal Change	53%	37%
Attention and Resources to the Poor	51	23
Societal Change and Attention and Resources to the Poor	26	12

a. All percentage differences are significant by X^2 ($p < .001$).
b. *N*s range from 1000 to 1020 in 1968 and from 667 to 675 in 1984.

1968 approved the emphasis on societal change as compared with 37 percent in 1984. Likewise, over half of the 1968 respondents favored devoting social work's resources to the problems of the poor compared with 23 percent in 1984. A greater proportion of social workers in 1968 approved of social work focusing on the goals of societal change and devoting resources primarily to the problems of the poor (26% in 1968 versus 12% in 1984). These differences were statistically significant.

Thus, despite their more social-structural conception of the causes of poverty than that of their predecessors, contemporary social workers are less committed to social work's devoting its institutional resources to the poor or to social change in their behalf.

This shift in goal orientation to a greater emphasis on individual adaptation and commitment to all social classes may possibly be attributed to the ascendancy of casework or psychotherapy as the primary social work method. As the number of private practitioners increases along with student aspirants to private practice (Rubin, Johnson, and DeWeaver 1986) fewer specialize in social policy, planning, or community organization. The consequence of these structural changes in the organization of social work may be to allow contemporary social workers to embrace more liberal or even radical explanations of the causes of social problems without a sense of occupational obligation to do anything about these problems.

Consistent with this explanation, social casework has received criticism for its goal of helping individuals adapt to the environment rather than engaging in broader processes of social change (Rein 1970; Galper 1975) and for developing technologies that "disengage the poor" (Cloward and Epstein 1965). (Later in this chapter, we examine the attitudes and behaviors of caseworkers and other practice groups within social work to determine whether practice methods makes a difference with regard to social activism.)

It may also be the case that contemporary social workers feel powerless to do anything about poverty. Hence, the failure of the Reagan Administration to commit itself to serving the needs of the poor may have contributed to a sense of futility on the part of most social workers about social work's contribution to solving the problem of poverty.

APPROVAL OF ACTIVIST STRATEGIES

Another aspect of social-worker activism deals with the means social workers will endorse to bring about social change. To measure their commitment to various strategies of social change, respondents in both surveys were asked to answer questions concerning their approval of a range of less to more activist social action strategies to change the public welfare system. Public welfare was chosen because it represents a traditional target of reform efforts in social work.

In his earlier study, Epstein (1969) devised a typology of social action strategies according to whether they were institutionalized or noninstitutionalized and whether they were based on consensus or conflict approaches. An institutionalized strategy involved "the use of a formally organized, publicly sanctioned structure for processing pressures for social change" whereas "a noninstitutionalized strategy operates outside formal and legitimated structures" (Epstein 1969:49). (For the various dimensions of this typology, see table 1.5.)

Specific strategies ranged from conducting studies of the needs of welfare recipients and providing expert testimony to actively organizing welfare recipients to conduct protests at the Department of Welfare.

By means of a Likert-type scale, respondents in both surveys were asked to indicate their approval or disapproval of each of these strategies when used by a group of "professional social workers acting as representatives of the profession" with the goal of obtaining "more government sponsored programs to help public welfare recipients."

Table 1.5 shows the percentage of the respondents in 1968 and 1984 who approved of social work's endorsing each change strategy.[1] The findings indicate that in 1968 and in 1984, social workers overwhelmingly accepted consensus strategies, both institutionalized (e.g., expert testimony) and noninstitutionalized (e.g., personal communication with public officials). In both periods over 80 percent of the social workers approved of consensus strategies. There were small but statistically significant declines in approval of conducting studies and giving expert testimony (95% in 1968 versus 90% in 1984) and providing direct services (90% in 1968 versus 84% in 1984).

As for approval of institutionalized conflict strategies, a large majority (86%) of social workers in both samples approved of encouraging welfare recipients to file complaints through formal channels. Fewer social workers, although still a majority, approved of the conflict strategy of campaigning for political candidates or working through political parties (78% in 1984 versus 68% in 1968). These differences were statistically significant.

By contrast, considerable disapproval was found among both sets of respondents over support for workers' involvement in noninstitutionalized

TABLE 1.5. Percentage in 1968 and 1984 Approving Each Strategy in Public Welfare Reform

Strategy	1968	1984
Institutionalized Consensus		
Studies and Expert Testimony	95%	90%
Coordination and Consensus	90	90
Noninstitutionalized Consensus		
Communication With Public Officials	95	96
Direct Provision of Services	90	84
Institutionalized Conflict		
Filing Formal Complaints	86	86
Political Campaigning	68	78
Noninstitutionalized Conflict		
Supporting Protest Groups	44	48
Organizing Protest Groups	28	41

a. All percentage differences are significant by X^2 ($p < .001$).
b. Ns range from 1010 to 1020 in 1968 and from 675 to 680 in 1984.

conflict strategies such as social protest. Thus, more than one-half of the social workers in both samples rejected the idea of the occupation offering support to protest groups or actively organizing protest demonstrations. Nevertheless, there was a statistically significant increase between 1968 and 1984 in the approval of the most controversial strategy, organizing protest action (41% in 1984 versus 28% in 1968).

Social workers in 1984 may have been less likely than those in 1968 to endorse the change strategies of conducting studies, giving expert testimony, and providing services directly because the abundance of existing studies and services then provided to welfare recipients was not successful in securing more programs. The finding that social workers today are more supportive of political campaigning to bring about social change is not surprising considering the National Association of Social Workers (NASW) support of social workers' involvement in political action. For example, in the 1984 presidential election, NASW sponsored voter registration drives as well as publicly endorsing a candidate for president for the first time in its history. A possible explanation for the finding that a greater proportion of social workers in 1984 approved of organizing protest actions may be that demonstrations have become more legitimized in social work. Supportive evidence for this view is found in reports in *NASW News* (October 1983; May 1986) that social workers have officially represented NASW at civil rights and anti-apartheid protest marches.

SOCIAL ACTION BEHAVIORS

Words are one thing, deeds are another. Consequently, there may be a gap between the social workers' espoused attitudes and the actions they are actually willing to take. To explore this distinction, we asked respondents in both surveys about their behaviors as well as their attitudes. To measure social workers' participation in different forms of social action, Epstein (1969) developed two different indices. The first, an index of institutionalized social action behavior, was based on respondents' indications that they had engaged in specific social actions, taken through institutionalized channels (e.g., visited a public official, gave public testimony, participated in an agency social action committee, etc.) during the past year. If they engaged in one or more of these behaviors in the past year, they were scored "high" on this index.

A second index, of noninstitutionalized social action behavior, was based on respondents' saying that they had engaged in at least one protest action in the past year (e.g., joined a protest demonstration, engaged in civil disobedience, etc.). Those saying that they had were scored "high" on this measure.

In her 1984 study, Reeser developed two additional measures—an index of electoral social action behavior and an index of professional social action behavior. For the first, respondents were asked to indicate which of a list of electoral activities (e.g., contributed money, attended public rallies, etc.) they have engaged in in the past five years. Those who had engaged in three actions were scored "high" on this measure.

For the second original index, Reeser asked her respondents about their involvement in social action activities specifically targeted to social work professionalization in the past year (e.g., licensing, social work lobbying). Those saying that they had engaged in one or more of these activities during the previous year were scored "high."

Table 1.6 shows the percentage of respondents in 1968 and 1984 scoring high on institutionalized and noninstitutionalized social action behavior and the percentage in 1984 scoring high on electoral and professional social action behavior.

TABLE 1.6. Percentage in 1968 and 1984 Scoring High on Social Action Behavior

Behavior	1968	1984
Institutionalized Social Action Behavior	47%	84%
Noninstitutionalized Social Action Behavior	29	17
Electoral Social Action Behavior	—	80
Professional Social Action Behavior	—	44

a. All percentage differences are significant by X^2 ($p < .001$).
b. N is 1020 in 1968 and and Ns range from 664 to 682 in 1984.

On the two measures for which we have the data to make historical comparisons, the differences between the sixties and the eighties are statistically significant. Thus, 84 percent of the social workers in 1984 scored high on such institutionalized social action behaviors as visiting a public official in the past year as contrasted with only 47 percent in 1968. Alternatively, the proportion of social workers engaged in noninstitutionalized forms of social action behavior such as protest demonstrations declined from 29 percent in 1968 to only 17 percent in 1984. In other words, while socially approved forms of political behavior nearly doubled, socially disapproved forms dropped by nearly one-half.

Looking at 1984 social workers' involvements in electoral politics, the vast majority (80%) of those surveyed in that year were highly involved in electoral activities. Of that same set of respondents, 44 percent participated actively in forms of behavior intended to augment the power and influence of social work, e.g., licensing, social work lobbying, and the like.

Comparison of some specific items on electoral and professional activism that both Reeser and Epstein included in their surveys suggests some of the historical changes that have occurred in social work since the 1960s. For example, in 1984, 64 percent of the respondents contributed money to a political campaign as compared with 36 percent in 1968. In 1984, 27 percent of the respondents canvassed or gave out leaflets as compared with 19 percent in 1968. In 1984, 35 percent of the respondents made efforts to influence the political participation of clients as compared with 10 percent in 1968.

Turning to professional political activities, in 1984, 33 percent of the respondents participated in social work lobbying for legislation as compared with 12 percent in 1968. In 1984, 28 percent of the social workers gave service on a social action committee of a professional association as compared with 6 percent in 1968. The differences between the two samples for all these items were statistically significant.

Historical comparison of the political behaviors of social workers suggests some fundamental shifts in the social action profile of social workers. Thus we see a clear movement toward active involvement in institutionalized and socially accepted forms of political behavior and away from noninstitutionalized, socially disapproved, conflict-based political approaches. The latter finding underscores the importance of studying behaviors as well as attitudes, since we noted earlier that social workers had expressed greater acceptance of social work involvement in organizing protest groups.

These patterns with regard to institutionalized forms of social, electoral, and professional action behavior are consistent with NASW's agenda, which encourages its membership to engage in social and political action as a "professional responsibility." Books used in social work schools reinforce this message and teach consensus-oriented, political skills (Alexander 1982; Haynes and Mickelson 1986).

In addition to the above, NASW has established a legislative action network (ELAN) so that members can maintain contact with their congressional representatives and pursue legislative priorities. A political action committee (PACE) was established to raise funds for the support of political candidates. Finally, NASW encourages its membership to be active in working for licensing and against declassification of social work jobs (NASW News June 1985). No comparable program existed in 1968. These efforts to gain licensing have become increasingly effective. Today, a majority of the NASW members work in jurisdictions with regulatory acts protective of social workers' rights to practice.

As for protest, we indicated earlier that NASW has made some effort to make it a more legitimate activity for "professionals," through its representation at various disarmament, anti-apartheid, and other protest demonstrations. This is perhaps reflected in the greater attitudinal acceptance of protest organizing in the 1984 sample. However, when we consider actual behaviors, NASW's membership has not taken up the protest banner very enthusiastically. In fact, quite the opposite appears to have happened.

SPECIALIZATION AND SOCIAL WORK ACTIVISM

So far the discussion has focused on the workers as a single group at two different points in time. This approach is consistent with a theoretical perspective on the professions and aspiring professions that views them as relatively homogeneous "communities within the community" (Goode 1957; Greenwood 1957) sharing common value commitments and political perspectives.

Diametrically opposed to this view is the "process model" proposed by Bucher and Strauss (1961:325) which suggests that rather than regarding professions as single, homogeneous communities it is more accurate to view them as "loose amalgamations of segments, pursuing different objectives in different manners and more or less deliberately held together under a common name at a particular time in history." From Bucher and Strauss' perspective, specialties are distinct in their histories, values, and by implication, their social activism.

This alternative theoretical approach raises two questions:

(1). Do practice groups within social work have differential commitments to activism?

(2). If so, have these commitments changed since the sixties?

To answer these questions, the social action attitudes and behaviors of caseworkers, group workers, and community organizers will next be examined, after which the social action commitments of social workers in private practice in 1984 and those working under different agency auspices will be considered.

Following the process approach, a review of the history, practice technology, agency affiliations, and ameliorative values of caseworkers would predispose them to be the least disposed to social activism of all social-work-practice groups. Thus, for example, the historical roots of casework are in the Charity Organization Society (COS) movement of the late nineteenth and early twentieth centuries. The COS approach to the poor was to investigate their backgrounds on a case-by-case basis to determine what moral deficiencies were the cause of their poverty (Trattner 1974). Clinical social work, a "direct descendent of the psychoanalytic perspective," has been accepted "as an integral component of social work" in recent years. It is a term often used to refer to casework (Briar 1987:394). Rein (1970:20–21) pointed out that the literature on casework has many references to helping clients conform in order to "achieve self-actualization and self-fulfillment."

By contrast, the historic roots of community organization support the prediction that community organizers would be most supportive of and involved in social and political activism. Originally allied with the social reformists of the settlement house movement (Trattner 1974), community organization as a social work specialization reached its peak during the War on Poverty and the civil rights movement. Community organization since the 1960s has encompassed both protest and advocacy (Brilland 1987:747).

Finally, one would predict that group workers would be more activist than caseworkers and less so than community organizers. This is because the group work segment is often regarded as polarized—split between a "remedial" clinical model and a more social-change oriented conception of group work (Papell and Rothman 1966). Group work had its historic roots in the settlement house movement. Wilson (1976) described the goals of group workers as to provide direct service to meet their clients' needs and social action to eliminate or ameliorate social problems. Today, however, group work tends to be clinical in nature because of the training received in social work schools and the funds available for social services (Middleman and Goldberg 1987:716, 726).

TABLE 1.7. Percentage in 1968 and 1984 Scoring High on Social Activism by Segment

	1968	*1968*
	Casework	*Group Work*
Activist Goals[b]	24%	36%
Public Welfare Conflict Approval[b]	37	59
Institutionalized Social Action Behavior	43[b]	64[b]
Noninstitutionalized Social Action Behavior	26[b]	51[b]
Electoral Social Action Behavior[a]	—	—
Professional Social Action Behavior	—	—
N =	731	107

a. $p < .05$.
b. $p < .001$.

Table 1.7 shows the percentage of caseworkers, group workers, and community organizers scoring high on each of the measures of social activism in 1968 and 1984. Identification with a practice group is determined by the respondent's area of specialization while in social work school.

As predicted, in 1968 and in 1984, caseworkers were least likely to support activist goals for social work, least likely to approve of conflict strategies in public welfare, and least likely to participate in both institutionalized and noninstitutionalized social action.

Also consistent with our expectations, community organizers of both time periods were generally more likely than caseworkers and group workers to endorse activist attitudes and engage in activist behavior. The one exception to this pattern is the finding that group workers were most likely to engage in protest-type behaviors in 1968 and least likely to do so in 1984.

These differences were not statistically significant in 1984 in regard to participation in institutionalized and noninstitutionalized activism based on the Chi-Square analysis. However, when the more sensitive Wilcoxon mean ranks test was used, the differences were statistically significant. And while caseworkers were significantly less activist than group workers

1968 *Community* *Organization*	*1984* *Casework*	*1984* *Group Work*	*1984* *Community* *Organization*
43%	33%	37%	69%
68	47	48	63
71[b]	83	83	88
32[b]	16	15	31
—	35	48	56
—	45	35	59
28	425	46	32

on all measures in 1968, there were no significant differences in social activism between these two practice segments in 1984. The one exception to this pattern is that group workers were significantly more active than caseworkers in electoral activities. No comparable data exist for 1968.

This set of findings suggests a decreasing differentiation of social work specializations in general and a remarkable similarity in the social-action profiles of caseworkers and group workers in recent years. One possible explanation for the blurring of differences between practice segments in recent years involves the kinds of agency settings in which most social workers are currently employed. So, for example, in 1968, 15 percent of the respondents in Epstein's study were employed in settings that supported activism (e.g., settlement houses, community action programs, community centers) as compared with only 2.3 percent of the respondents in 1984.

This markedly lower proportion of social workers in activist settings is likely to be attributed to the dismantling of most of the War on Poverty programs and the preponderance of social workers seeking employment in mental health agencies.

Another possible explanation for the blurring of distinctions between caseworkers and group workers is that many social work schools are combining casework and group work training into a "generic" direct service concentration designed to prepare practitioners who can use both methods. Despite the lip service given to equal weighting of the two practice orientations, the actual training and fieldwork experience associated with it is generally "weighted toward work with individuals and families" (Middleman and Goldberg 1987:716). Consequently, group work content is decreasing and quite possibly along with it the unique social-action orientation of that segment.

Along with generic training, today's group workers are practicing a more "remedial" or clinical model rather than the traditional "developmental" model. The "developmental" model contrasts sharply with the clinical practice of social work in that it focuses on "social functionality rather than pathology" and on "self-actualization rather than treatment or cure" (Tropp 1971:1247). Currently, the "remedial" model of group work seems to have gained ascendancy. Funds for social services are focused on clients with problems, particularly mental health and medical. "Little money . . . is available for outreach and for services to people believed to be 'normal' " (Middleman and Goldberg 1987:726). The latter group were traditionally targets for citizenship training and more politically activist models of group work practice.

Looking at changes within practice segments across the years is also instructive. Our findings indicate that caseworkers in 1984 were almost twice as active in institutionalized social action behaviors than they were in 1968 (an increase of 40%) and slightly less involved in noninstitutionalized behaviors such as protest (a decline of 10%). Group workers, on the other hand, had markedly increased their participation in institutionalized forms of activism (by 29%) and dramatically decreased their participation in protest (by 36%). The differences were statistically significant. Finally, although community organizers had significantly increased their commitment to activist goals by 26 percent, their increase in institutionalized social action behaviors had increased the least of all segments (17%) and was not statistically significant. Their involvement in protest had remained virtually the same.

Since community organizers were highest in institutionalized social action behaviors in 1968, they had the least room to increase along this dimension.

Nevertheless, in 1984 they remain the highest in their participation in social action efforts in behalf of social work professionalization and in electoral politics. Caseworkers were significantly least activist along the dimension of electoral activism, while group workers, as predicted, were somewhere in between. Group workers were least activist in their participation in professional activism and caseworkers were in between. The differences were not significant.

AUSPICE AND ACTIVISM

Considering the context or auspice within which social workers practice their specializations, one would assume that private as opposed to agency-based practitioners would be least involved in social activism, with the exception of licensing and vendorship campaigns which are intended to gain sanction for independent social work practice. Thus, it was predicted that social workers in private practice would be more involved in professional activism and less involved in and supportive of other types of activism than would social workers employed in other auspices.

Table 1.8 shows the percentage of social workers in private practice,

TABLE 1.8. Percent Scoring High on Social Activism by Auspice (1984)

	Private Practice	Public	Voluntary: Sectarian	Voluntary: Nonsectarian
Activist Goals	30%	40%	46%	44%
Public Welfare Conflict Approval	53	45	57	51
Institutionalized Social Action Behavior	89	83	91	87
Noninstitutionalized Social Action Behavior[a]	18	13	23	26
Electoral Social Action Behavior[a]	44	31	46	40
Professional Social Action Behavior	58	42	43	44
$N =$	79	327	44	120

a. $p < .01$.

public, voluntary sectarian, and voluntary nonsectarian agencies scoring high on each index of social action behavior in 1984. Comparable data analysis could not be done for the 1968 sample, when only 3 percent indicated being in private practice. In the 1984 sample population however, 12 percent so indicated.

As predicted, private practitioners in 1984 were most likely to participate in such professional activities as licensing efforts and relatively low in their involvement in protest behaviors. They also were least likely to approve of activist goals for social work although the Chi-Square difference was not statistically significant. When the more sensitive Wilcoxon mean ranks test was used the difference was significant.

Contrary to the prediction, however, they were not less approving of conflict strategies in public welfare and there were no significant differences in participation in institutionalized activism. And, they were more likely than social workers employed in public and voluntary nonsectarian agencies to be engaged in electoral politics.

Private practitioners were not less active than other social workers in the majority of the social action measures. The findings may be a consequence of comparing private practitioners to relatively nonactivist case-workers and group workers who were included in the other auspices.

Alternatively, it may be that private practitioners are relatively activist in their orientations although their political ideologies may be relatively "conservative." In Levenstein's (1964) study of private practitioners, he found that they were more active in the community and in NASW than agency workers. The agency workers in Levenstein's study apparently felt that social action was the responsibility of their agencies rather than themselves.

The finding that private practitioners were more active in licensing efforts, lobbying, and electoral activism is supported by other research. Wallace (1977:97) stated that they have put much time and money into licensing efforts because they "felt illegitimate outside of their agencies." A large proportion of private practitioners hold office in NASW (Wallace 1982).

Surprisingly, social workers employed in the public sector were the least activist in their attitudes and behaviors. The Hatch Act's prohibitions against involvement in politics probably accounts for their lesser involvement in electoral activism and protest actions, and the lesser acceptance of conflict strategies in public welfare might also be explained in terms of public workers' institutional interests. Since they are most likely to work directly for, have a contract with, or work in collaboration with the Department of Welfare, their institutional interests, livelihoods, and practice would be threatened if social workers were to organize massive protests against public welfare agencies.

SUMMARY

Thus far our study findings indicate that since the sixties there have been significant changes in social workers' social action attitudes and behaviors, their conceptions of goals for their profession, and their attitudes toward poverty and the poor, generally, and consistent with our expectations, social workers in 1968 seemed more committed to social work's involvement in social change and serving the poor and, thus, more approving of an activist goal orientation. In addition, they were more actively involved in social protest.

Contrary to expectations, however, social workers in the sixties held more individualized and less social-structural views of the causes of poverty and were, even then, not primarily invested in serving poor clients in their agencies. Thus, even in the late sixties, the majority preferred serving all income groups equally. Moreover, even though they were more likely to be engaged in protest as individuals, social workers in the 1960s did not endorse conflict strategies for the occupation as a whole and gave little approval to social workers' involvement in direct action protest. Consequently, they were more likely to be involved in institutionalized forms of activism than in protest.

Paradoxically, social workers in 1984 were more likely to endorse structural explanations for the existence of poverty. And while they were more likely than those in 1968 to approve of the use of protest for "social work as a profession," they still preferred consensus strategies for social change. The findings also indicate that contemporary social workers are much more likely to be engaged in noncontroversial actions such as visiting public officials, working in political campaigns, and working for the licensing of social workers. In addition, they are less likely to want to serve the poor primarily or to endorse an activist goal orientation for social work than their predecessors in the 1960s. Thus, despite their attribution of poverty to systemic causes, social workers in the 1980s apparently do not regard the elimination of poverty as a priority of their occupation. Instead, they view the role of social work as helping individuals of all social classes to adapt to the environment. The above findings strongly suggest that today's social workers hold political attitudes and behave politically in ways that are consistent with Souflée's (1977) notion of social work as a "consenting profession" integrated with and supportive of the political and social class system. On the other hand, social workers in the sixties were more likely to view social work as a "dissenting profession" (Souflée 1977) involved in broad movements for social change and the elimination of poverty. These differences, however, should not obscure the fact that both groups preferred and engaged in noncontroversial change strategies and work with a mixed clientele.

Additional findings support the use of a "process" approach to the prediction of differences in the social activism of social workers in the sixties and in the eighties. Thus, social workers may be placed into distinctive practice segments with associated differences in their commitments. Nevertheless, there is some evidence to suggest that the differences between two of these segments—casework and group work—have become greatly diminished.

Overall, caseworkers in 1968 and 1984 were both the largest and the least activist. This is true for both goal orientations and social action strategies, and for both institutionalized and noninstitutionalized behavior. The prevalence of caseworkers in social work and the social action orientations they hold may give the impression that social work as an institution is inherently "conservative."

Chapter 3 is concerned with the extent to which social work has become increasingly professionalized in the 1980s. One of the issues we will consider in chapter 4 is whether the data support the assumption that the decrease in noninstitutionalized activism of social workers is a consequence of the greater professionalization of social workers in recent years.

But before we consider these complex questions, let us turn, in chapter 2, to a further analysis of the similarities and differences in activism between social workers of the 1960s and those of the 1980s by considering the impact of the demographic and social characteristics that social workers bring to the field.

2

Background Characteristics and Social Work Activism

In the previous chapter we compared the activist attitudes and behaviors of social workers in the sixties and in the eighties. We then looked at the relative degrees of social activism of major segments within social work during these dramatically different periods in social work history.

Above and beyond what was occurring within social work in the sixties and eighties, major changes were taking place in the society at large. The growth of the women's movement, the rise and decline of the civil rights and anti-poverty movements, the political mobilization of the elderly, and the activation of college campuses with the "new left" and anti-Vietnam War movements and the subsequent depoliticization of college campuses when the war ended were just some of the changes that took place between these decades.

These movements had profound influences on women, people of color, the aged and the young, and others who were politically involved in them. Even if only indirectly, they powerfully effected those who were not actively involved.

As an institution which is part of the larger society, social work is likely to be effected by dramatic changes such as these. Nevertheless, within the context of the debate about social work activism and its determinants, the political involvements and movement-relevant background characteristics of social workers are generally ignored. Treated as such, they remain "latent social identities" (Gouldner 1958). This is especially noteworthy because demographic characteristics have been shown to affect the political commitments and activism of people in every walk of life.

In this chapter, we consider the changing relationships between the background characteristics and political identities that social workers bring to the field and their activism. More precisely, we look at the effects of gender, race and religion, age, and political party affiliation.

SOCIAL-CLASS ORIGINS AND SOCIAL WORK ACTIVISM

Much theorizing has been done concerning the effects of intergenerational mobility on political attitudes and behavior. (See Hamilton 1966; Lipset and Bendix 1960; Lopreato 1967). Epstein (1969) examined the consequences of class origins in his study of social workers. He measured the intergenerational mobility patterns of his sample by classifying the educational and occupational ranks of respondents' fathers using the Hollingshead "Two Factor Index" (1965). Approximately 12 percent of his respondents came from the lowest class, 31 percent from the lower-middle class, 26 percent from the middle class, 17 percent from the upper-middle class, and 14 percent from the highest class. He found no significant relation between class of origin and social activism. He suggested that since social workers come primarily from the lower-middle and middle classes, they "experience relatively similar degrees of economic and political power" (p. 178). Epstein found that other background characteristics are more important in differentiating the activism of social workers. Thus, Reeser (1986) did not collect data on the class origins of social workers in her sample. Therefore, there can be no comparison of the effects of social class in social workers' social action attitudes and behaviors in the sixties and eighties.

GENDER AND SOCIAL WORK ACTIVISM

Until relatively recently, the social work literature on activism and popular discussion of this topic among social workers has tended to ignore the possible impact of gender on the involvements of rank-and-file social workers. The one context in which gender-related activism has been discussed involves the historic contribution that activist women made to the evolution of social work. Thus, for example, Trattner (1974) and Vandiver (1980) trace the beginnings of social work to the activism of women who were

involved in social change efforts in their roles as charity workers, reform-
ers, and suffragettes.

At present, the "gender lens" of feminist social workers is focused
primarily on the question of whether institutional sexism exists within social
work and, if it does, how it affects women in social work and the female
clients they serve (Weick 1980; Sancier 1980; Meyer 1980; Cummings
1980; Kravetz 1976; Kravetz 1982; Longres and Bailey 1979; Tolman et
al. 1986).

Nevertheless, over the last several decades, the political impact of
gender in American society has been widely researched by political and
social scientists. Their focus has been primarily on political participation,
narrowly defined as voting behavior. Reviewing this line of research en-
quiry, Milbrath (1965:135) perhaps prematurely concluded that "the finding
that men are more likely to participate in politics than women is one of the
most thoroughly substantiated in social science." He did note, however,
that this difference was gradually decreasing because of industrialization
and changing social roles.

In their cross-cultural study of the political attitudes and behaviors of
citizens in five countries, Almond and Verba (1965) found that relative to
women in other countries, American women tended to be more politically
active in their communities, politically informed, and felt competent to exert
influence over their political representatives. However, for all the indices
they employed, men (in all countries) were more committed to political
activism than women.

Less than two decades later, in their study of American women, Baxter
and Lansing (1983) found that, although men are more politically active on
other dimensions, the difference in voting rates between women and men
in 1980 was negligible. They attribute this decreased difference to greater
equality of education, income, and labor force participation. And, by 1984,
according to the last census survey, the voter turnout rate of women was
1.8 percent higher than that of men (Cavanaugh 1985:15). Despite their
increasing political participation, a variety of gender-based reasons have
been offered to "explain" why women were less politically involved than
men. Some blamed women, some blamed men, some blamed society, and
some blamed all of the above.

Hence, in Kirkpatrick's (1974:19) study of why so few women held or
sought political office at that time, the following explanations were offered:
psychological differences between men and women that are determined by
biology; cultural norms dictating that politics is "man's work"; and the

barring of women "from power by a ruling class bent on maintaining its hegemony."

Overall, the reason most commonly cited by political scientists for gender differences in voting behavior and political office-holding was different patterns of socialization for men and women. According to this reasoning, men and women were socialized to believe that men alone were competent to make political decisions and to hold significant political positions in society (Berelson, Lazarsfeld, and McPhee 1954; Almond and Verba 1965; Baxter and Lansing 1983).

Most of the foregoing studies of the general populace define political activism in terms of electoral participation alone. By contrast, this and other studies of the political activism of various occupational groups define activism more broadly to include forms of political behavior that extend beyond voting and include occupationally relevant social action. Nevertheless, they shed light on the differential (or nondifferential) effects of gender.

So, for example, in a study of the relative militancy (e.g., strike behavior) of male and female members of the National Education Association, Wagenaar (1974) found that female teachers were generally less active than their male counterparts. In another study of school teachers, conducted a year later, Fox and Wince (1976) found the same pattern. They attributed the gender differences in activism to greater male aggression and to the relative deprivation that men experience when, as primary wage earners, they compare their salaries to those of men with comparable education in more lucrative occupations.

Shifting societal arrangements, the use of different definitions and measures of activism by researchers, and the impact of different occupational experiences on workers all suggest caution in generalizing about male/female differences in activism. Nonetheless, political scientists have tended to perpetuate myths and stereotypes about women as being inherently apolitical. These myths and stereotypes are especially problematic to the degree that they result in a self-fulfilling prophecy that limits the extent to which women regard themselves and are regarded by society as rightfully equal and full participants in the political process.

Recognizing this problem, Bourque and Grossholtz (1974:227–228) identified four common and fallacious assumptions in political theory and research. These are: (1) "the assumption of male dominance" so that the monopoly on political power that men have is not questioned; (2) the assumption that male patterns of political expression represent ideal political behavior; (3) the assumption that women have a "commitment to the eternal feminine" which restricts women to the roles of wives, mothers, and political helpmates; and finally (4) the "fudging of the footnotes," which involves making unsubstantiated statements about previous research based on the assumption that women are apolitical.

As for the determinants of activism, caution also must be exercised in concluding that women are less likely to be primary wage earners, less committed to their careers, or feel less deprived because of low salaries than men. Thus, recent research has shown that an increasing proportion of women are sole wage earners who are highly committed to maintaining their careers (Iglehart 1979; Yohalem 1979).

Finally, feelings of relative deprivation are not limited to men. In fact, in many occupational contexts women are justified in feeling doubly deprived. First, because female dominated occupations receive less pay than male dominated occupations (Baker 1978; Blau 1978; Treiman and Hartmann 1981; Perlman and Grune 1982). Second, because females within any given occupation are likely to receive less pay and status than men (Bielby 1985; Epstein 1981; Fox 1987).

Although there exist justifiable criticisms of the assumptions made about women and activism in social science theory and research, there is general agreement that in the sixties women were less politically active than men. In the eighties, however, these differences seemed to have diminished somewhat. Thus, the women's movement, educational and occupational changes, higher rates of divorce, and single parenthood are all likely to have contributed to substantial changes in the social-political environment of women and men.

This raises the question of whether these environmental influences are reflected in gender differences in the activism of social workers in the two eras.

Testing the Effects of Gender

The previous discussion of gender and political activism suggests that male social workers in the sixties were significantly more activist than their female counterparts. Consequently, one would predict that in the 1968 sample of NASW members, men would be more likely than women to endorse activist goals, to approve of conflict strategies in public welfare, and to participate in institutionalized and noninstitutionalized social action behavior.

In addition, the previous discussion suggests a greater similarity between men and women in their activism in the eighties. More precisely, one would predict that in the 1984 sample, male social workers would not be significantly more activist in their endorsement of goals or conflict strategies. Neither would they be significantly more activist in their institutionalized, noninstitutionalized, electoral, or professionally oriented activist behaviors. There is no comparable data on electoral or professional activism for 1968.

To begin our gender analysis, table 2.1 shows us that the relative proportions of men and women was very much the same in 1968 and in 1984. In the earlier sample population, 68 percent were women as compared with 71 percent in 1984. This ratio of women to men has been fairly consistent within social work over the last decade[1] and supports our claim to the representativeness of our two sample populations.

As for our first prediction, concerning gender and activism, table 2.1 shows that in 1968 male social workers were more likely than females to endorse activist goals (32% vs. 23%), to approve conflict strategies in

TABLE 2.1. Percent Scoring High on Social Activism by Sex in 1968 and 1984

	1968		1984	
Measures of Activism	*Female*	*Male*	*Female*	*Male*
Activist Goals	23%[a]	32%[a]	40%	36%
Public Welfare Conflict Approval	36[b]	48[b]	47	42
Institutionalized Social Action Behavior	42[b]	59[b]	84	84
Noninstitutionalized Social Action Behavior	26[b]	36[b]	16	19
Electoral Social Action Behavior	—	—	36	33
Professional Social Action Behavior[c]	—	—	39[b]	57[b]
N =	610	286	485	197

a. $p < .01$
b. $p < .001$
c. Data on professional and political social action behavior are available only for 1984.

public welfare reform (48% vs. 36%), to participate in both institutionalized (59% vs. 42%) and noninstitutionalized forms of social action behavior (36% vs. 26%). (These differences were all statistically significant.)

In support of our second prediction, table 2.1 shows that in 1984 male social workers no longer differed significantly in their activism from their female colleagues on five out of six measures. In fact, on three out of six (activist goals, endorsement of conflict strategies, and electoral behavior), women were slightly more activist than men.

Only one statistically significant difference ran counter to our prediction: male social workers in 1984 were significantly more likely than females to have engaged in professionally oriented activist behavior such as lobbying for licensure (57% vs. 39%).

Closer analysis of the data from the eighties revealed, however, that men with 10 years or more experience, trained in casework, and still in direct-service roles were most activist on this dimension. A plurality of these men (44%) were employed in public agencies. For these men, possibly locked into direct-service positions after 10 years or more in the field, dissatisfaction with their career immobility may lead to a sense of relative deprivation which is expressed in licensing and lobbying activity against declassification. This form of activism is designed to support the upward mobility of social work as a profession and to protect it against deprofessionalization. As such, it represents an alternative, collective strategy for career mobility and the maintenance of job security. The second largest group of these men were private practitioners (18%) who may work for licensing to gain sanction for their practice.

For those social workers with less than 10 years experience, trained in group work or community organization, and working in other than direct service roles, however, there was no significant difference between men and women in their involvement in professionally oriented lobbying or licensing efforts. Hence for all but a particular group of male social workers, on a single aspect of social activism, women in social work in the eighties were every bit as activist as men.

Since we have no comparable data regarding gender differences in licensing and lobbying efforts by social workers in the 1968 sample we have no way of knowing whether this gender differential in professionally oriented activist behavior has increased, remained constant, or diminished since the sixties.

Direct comparison within gender categories in the 1968 and 1984 samples indicates that in instances where there was an increase in activism from the sixties to the eighties, women increased more than men. Women increased their commitment to activist goals by 17 percent compared with 4 percent for men. The difference for females was statistically significant ($p < .001$). The women nearly doubled their participation in institutionalized activism in 1984 (an increase of 42%), while males increased their activism by only 25 percent. Women decreased their participation in protest less than men (-10% vs. -17%). The differences were statistically significant ($p < .001$).

These findings are consistent with what we know about what happened in the women's movement and in social work since the sixties, when the movement first sought to obtain economic, political, and social self-determination for women. This was the time when, in the words of Bella Abzug (1984:110),

> the post-suffrage women's organizations moved from their second stage of civic-minded, nonpartisan, "good government" political activity into the third stage of mass political activism. This change has had a significant impact on women's political behavior . . . .

For the first time since the suffrage movement, women had developed a sophisticated organizational structure to represent their interests as well as a presence in national politics (Gelb and Palley 1982). This political mobilization of American women led to the passage of Title IX of the Education Amendment (which prohibited sex discrimination in federally assisted programs and in the field of education) in 1972, the Equal Credit Opportunity Act in 1974, and the Pregnancy Disability Act in 1978.

In the seventies it was not just women's rights groups such as the National Organization of Women (NOW), that were involved in feminist legislative victories. These victories were shared by feminist congresswomen, lobbyists, and journalists, as well as traditional women's groups such as the National Federation of Business Women and Professional Women's Clubs. The political mobilization of women of the seventies culminated in the "unprecedented grass-roots lobbying effort mounted by NOW and other women's groups" during the debate on the Equal Rights Amendment (ERA) extension, which passed in 1978 (Kolker 1983:211).

Although the resurgence of feminism began in the sixties, the movement became much more cohesive and received more broad-based support in the seventies. Many women who participated in the civil rights and New Left movements in the previous decade were disillusioned and radicalized by the experience of being treated as subordinates and having feminist issues "neglected and scorned" (Gelb and Palley 1982:18–19). Educated and middle-class women became more aware of major discrepancies between expectation and reality for women. In the early seventies women's rights groups created policy networks with traditional women's groups to gain congressional passage of the ERA and these networks have remained intact. By the late seventies many of the once "radical" ideas of the women's liberation groups (e.g., lesbian rights) were supported by many feminists (Gelb and Palley 1982).

The broad-based support by women for efforts to change and strengthen the status of women clearly had its effect on social work organizations in the seventies. In that decade the first women's caucuses were formed in NASW and in the Council on Social Work Education (CSWE). Female social workers, who were previously ridiculed for suggesting that sexism was institutionalized in social work, with persistent effort won the following victories: (1) NASW and CSWE created standing committees on women's issues; (2) NASW's affirmative action programs required proportional representation of women in its offices; and (3) CSWE guidelines for accreditation required that women's issues be incorporated into the curricula of schools of social work (Sancier 1980:189–190).

Our empirical findings suggest that these societal and organizational changes of the sixties and seventies had a significant impact on the activism of rank-and-file social workers in the eighties such that women became equal to men in their activism and showed dramatic increases in their commitment to activist goals and participation in institutionalized activism. And since social workers are more likely to be women, these findings auger well for the future commitment of social work to social reform efforts.

AGE AND SOCIAL ACTIVISM

Another background characteristic which is generally assumed to be associated with political and social activism is age. Thus, for example, a number of studies of political participation have reported that older persons were more likely to vote and to have stronger party identification than younger persons (Milbrath 1965). These studies explained that increased age was associated with greater integration in the community and thus greater electoral activism. The reason offered for increasing party ties with increasing age was that, over time, "partisanship solidifies with exposure to the party system" (Nie, Verba, and Petrocik 1979:62). These studies tended to split respondents into younger and older groups.

Studies which focus on the political effects of stages in the life cycle and the physiological aspects of aging are more likely to utilize age ranges, rather than young versus old dichotomies, to analyze the relationship between age and political participation. These studies have demonstrated a curvilinear relationship between age and political behavior.

Thus, Milbrath (1965:134) described the "typical curve," which indicates that "participation rises gradually with age, reaches its peak and levels off in the forties and fifties, and gradually declines above sixty." The most common explanation for this curvilinear pattern is based on the "start-up" and "slow-down" theories. They suggest that young people have the problem of "start-up" in their electoral and political party involvements because they are likely to be mobile and have little stake in the politics of any particular community. By implication, such a theory would explain why the activism of younger people is channeled through noninstitutionalized structures such as protest groups.

Integration into a community develops gradually and when it occurs institutionalized forms of political participation rises. As people reach advanced age, however, it is theorized that political participation decreases, because older people "slow-down." Consequently, they withdraw from their previous political involvements because of retirement, loss of income, and physical disability (Verba and Nie 1981).

Supporting these theories, a number of studies from the forties to the sixties found the elderly lowest in their sense of political efficacy (defined as the belief that one's political action does have, or could have, an impact upon the political process) and in their belief that one ought to participate in politics (Schmidhauser 1970). These attitudinal findings were used to support the proposition that the elderly inevitably disengage from the political process.

Even in the sixties however, there was disagreement in the literature as to whether the elderly were, in fact, politically indifferent and about the extent to which there was a decrease in political participation in the later years (Campbell et al. 1964; Glenn and Grimes 1968). Claims of low interest and low efficacy were challenged.

In a study of the 1960 presidential election, Campbell et al. (1964), found no relationship between age and a sense of political efficacy or citizenship. Verba and Nie (1981) found that when education and socioeconomic status were controlled there was no concomitant decrease for the elderly in voting behavior. In the case of more active forms of participation (e.g., campaigning for candidates, contacting local officials) there was only a slight decline with age. They concluded that any differences in participation were more likely to be a result of education and income differences in their sample rather than a consequence of aging.

Some observers even reported that political interest actually increased with age to replace loss of job and family involvement (Glenn and Grimes 1968; Weaver 1981).

Although there was no consensus among political scientists on the effects of age on political participation, there was agreement that people tend to become more "conservative" as they grow older. This popular belief is firmly rooted in conventional wisdom as well.

Testing the truth of this belief, Glenn published a review of the previous 20 years of national survey data in 1981. He reported that the data "rather consistently show elderly people as a whole to be more conservative than middle-aged people and the latter to be more conservative than young adults" (Glenn 1981:24). Among the "conservative" characteristics correlated with age in these studies were cautiousness about change, opposition to school desegregation, identification with the Republican party, and voting for conservative candidates for public office. These findings suggest that increasing age brings greater integration in the socioeconomic system and, thus, greater commitment to the status quo.

Although there were several studies published in the political science literature concerning age, political activism, and ideological conservatism in the general population, only a few studies were published concerning the relationships among these factors within specific occupational groups. Nevertheless, one would assume that what held true for the general population was also true for occupations.

Supporting this assumption, Centers (1961:165) found that among professionals, semiprofessionals, and white collar workers age was associated with "conservative politico-economic orientations." Conservatism was measured by an attitude index with items concerning labor management relations, government ownership of business, and values of individualism vs. collectivism.

Two studies of school teachers examined the relationship between age and union activity. Wagenaar (1974:375) found that there was a slight inverted U-shaped, curvilinear relationship between age and militancy (e.g., going on strike) for teachers who belonged to the American Federation of

Teachers (AFT). However, for members of the National Education Association (NEA), there was a linear, positive association between years of experience and militant activism. His explanation for the latter, unexpected finding that older and more experienced teachers were more active was that they had seniority and support from other staff members. He conjectured that "such a respected and status-secure position may be a prerequisite to a high level of professional activism."

Similarly, Divers (1980) found that older teachers were more involved in union activities and participated more in strikes than younger teachers.

Generalizations then, concerning age and activism can be equally as risky as those concerning gender. For example, Glenn (1981) critiqued research that supported the aging and conservatism thesis on the basis of the varying measures and definitions of conservatism used in different studies and the absence of convincing evidence of the effects of the biological, social, and psychological aging processes. His argument was that the aging process, per se, may not account for the differences in conservatism between age groups.

Instead, he asserted that age-related differences in political attitudes and beliefs are the result of the different formative experiences that the young and the old have had in their lives. This explanation is based on the different historical circumstances that shaped the political perspectives of different birth cohorts rather than on the aging process.

Thus, older people tend to have less formal education on the average, and conservatism tends to vary inversely with the amount of education. The aging process itself, Glenn contends, may have little to do with increasing conservatism.

Following Glenn's reasoning, voting studies and studies of other forms of political activism may be criticized because they have tended to be ahistorical, ignoring the historical context in which their sample populations were embedded. Simply stated, just as women have become more politically self-conscious since the sixties, so have the elderly. As a result, researchers and theoreticians who ignore changing historical conditions and period influences and who seek generalizations about age and activism that are true for all time are likely to go astray.

Finally, Wagenaar's (1974) and Diver's (1980) studies of school teachers, their unions, and their professional associations caution us about ignoring occupational and organizational influences on the relationship between age and activism.

Assessing Effects of Age

Although our brief literature review revealed some disagreement as to whether the aging process, per se, brought greater ideological conservatism, or whether conservatism was correlated with aging because of the intervening of effects such factors as education, cultural influences, and the like, there was general agreement (at least into the seventies) that the elderly were more politically conservative than the general population.

As for institutionalized forms of political behavior such as voting, it was generally agreed that an inverted U curve was as descriptive of the relationship between age and activism. Noninstitutionalized activist behavior was, however, more problematic. On the one hand, the research on ideological conservatism of the general population and on professionals and semi-professionals in the sixties would suggest an inverse relationship with age. On the other hand, data on school teachers' strikes in the seventies suggest quite the opposite.

And, as with gender, historical movements between the sixties and the eighties such as the political mobilization of the elderly suggest caution in generalizing from one decade to the other. Finally, it must be remembered that many of the people who were involved in "the Movement" in the sixties are today contemplating their retirements.

On the basis of the above discussion, one would predict that older social workers in the 1968 sample would have been less likely to endorse activist goals, approve conflict strategies, and participate in noninstitutionalized activist behaviors than their younger colleagues. As for institutionalized social action behaviors, one would predict a curvilinear relationship, increasing through middle-age and decreasing in the later years.

For social workers in the 1984 sample, predictions are more daunting. Can we assume that the aging process among social workers inevitably leads to lesser militancy? Or, have the historical experiences of the sixties remained with older social workers in the eighties? Only a look at the data will tell us.

Table 2.2 describes the relationships between age and activism of the social workers sampled in 1968. In this table, three out of four of our findings are consistent with our predictions. Two out of four were statistically significant.

Contrary to our prediction, we see that with increasing age social workers in 1968 were no less likely to support activist goals of social change in behalf of the poor. However, as to their endorsement of conflict strategies

TABLE 2.2. Percent Scoring High on Social Activism by Age (1968)

Measures of Activism	*Under 30*	*30–39*	*40–49*	*50–59*	*60 and Above*
Activist Goals	22%	27%	30%	22%	25%
Public Welfare Conflict Approval[a]	50	48	37	33	23
Institutionalized Social Action Behavior[a]	30	45	52	56	49
Noninstitutionalized Social Action Behavior	33	34	24	29	18
N =	142	238	225	215	71

a. $p < .001$.

to bring about these changes, we find that 50 percent of those social workers under 30 years of age do so as compared to only 23 percent of those 60 and above. (This finding is significant at the .001 level of significance.) Similarly (but not statistically significant), 33 percent of the social workers surveyed in 1968 participated in protest-type activities in the previous year as compared with 18 percent of those 60 and above.

Finally, with regard to more socially approved, institutionalized activism, we see the predicted curvilinear relationship. This form of political involvement increases from 30 percent for those under 30, to 56 percent for those in their fifties, and declines to 49 percent for those 60 and above. (This pattern is significant at the .001 level.)

The picture is somewhat different in 1984. Slight differences in the age categories used in the two surveys preclude exact comparison, but the age categories are close enough to compare patterns. And, some of the patterns are quite different.

Thus, although table 2.3 reveals a similar pattern of "nonrelationship" between age and endorsement of activist goals as was found in the sixties, there was no corresponding decline in the endorsement of conflict strategies by older social workers in the eighties, nor was there an inverse relationship between age and protest behavior as there was in the sixties. Interestingly, it is the social workers who were between 41 and 50 years

TABLE 2.3. Percent Scoring High on Social Activism by Age (1984)

Measures of Activism	21–30	31–40	41–50	51–60	Over 60
Activist Goals	34%	45%	29%	43%	44%
Public Welfare Conflict Approval	48	51	44	46	44
Institutionalized Social Action Behavior[a]	82	82	85	88	93
Noninstitutionalized Social Action Behavior	20	14	12	25	22
Electoral Social Action Behavior[b]	23	35	31	54	46
Professional Social Action Behavior[b]	30	43	45	56	59
N =	122	238	161	106	54

a. $p < .05$.
b. $p < .001$.

of age in 1984 who scored lowest on these more militant measures of activism. These respondents probably entered social work during the fifties and the McCarthy era.

As to the remaining relatively noncontroversial forms of activism, we find a direct linear relationship between age and institutionalized and profession-oriented action behavior. On the measure of institutionalized activism, 82 percent of the social workers 40 and under scored high as compared with 93 percent of those over 60. Thirty percent of the social workers who are 30 and under scored high on such actions as pro-licensing lobbying as compared with 59 percent of those over 60. We find the inverted U shaped, curvilinear relationship between age and electoral involvement with a slight decline in the curve for the 41 to 50 age group. However, social workers over 60 still score higher on electoral activism than social workers 50 and under. (All three of these relationships between age and institutionalized types of activism are statistically significant.)

Finally, to determine whether elderly social workers in the eighties were more or less activist than their younger colleagues a Wilcoxon Mean Rank Test was applied to two groups of social workers (those 60 and under and those over 60) for each measure of activism (see table 2.4). On the more militant measures of activism, older social workers were found to be no less activist than their younger colleagues. Moreover, on the more socially approved measures of institutionalized, electoral, and professional social action behaviors, "elderly" social workers were found to be considerably more activist than there more "youthful" compeers. (These differences were each significant at the .05 level.)

Again, comparing the two decades, older social workers in the sixties appeared to be less accepting of conflict strategies and less involved in protest than their younger colleagues. The eighties showed no comparable trend toward greater conservatism with age. As for age and endorsement of activist goals, the findings for the two decades are quite similar.

In addition, direct comparison within the over 60 age category in the 1984 and 1968 samples indicates that older social workers in 1984 greatly increased in all types of activism except for protest actions. For example, 49 percent participated in institutionalized activism in 1968; 93 percent did so in 1984. The differences were statistically significant. There was a slight decrease in their participation in noninstitutionalized activism (− 4%).

The findings within and across the decades show us why it is so important to keep the historical, political, occupational, and organizational environment in mind when making assertions about the impact of age on activism. So, for example, we know that the political and social environments of the past four decades have been vastly different. In addition, it must be remembered that while at any single point in time social workers share the same historical moment, they come to it with vastly different formative experiences.

TABLE 2.4. Wilcoxon Mean Ranks on Social Activism by Age (1984)

Measures of Activism	60 and Under	Over 60	Result
Institutionalized Social Action Behavior	336	393	.05
Electoral Social Action Behavior	327	381	.05
Professional Social Action Behavior	336	390	.05
N =	627	54	

For example, in the 1968 sample, social workers over 60 had grown up in the twenties. At that time government was closely allied with business, social welfare legislation was at a standstill, the country was hostile to everything foreign, and patriotism was at its zenith. Leuchtenburg (1958:205) characterized it as a time when "every effort toward social change was condemned as unAmerican." Facing retirement, and having grown up in a relatively conservative society, these social workers were confronted by a liberal, if not to say "radical" political climate in 1968.

Contrast their personal experience with older social workers in the 1984 sample. They grew up during the thirties. During their formative years, the economic upheaval of the Depression forced major changes in virtually every social, economic, and political institution that existed. The New Deal changed the role of the federal government from that of a neutral arbiter to an entity that takes responsibility for the social welfare of its citizens. During this period, emphasis was placed on collective action to bring about change and a more just society (Leuchtenburg 1963).

Thus, it may be that no declining relationship was found between age and militancy in the eighties because older social workers grew up in a liberal political climate during a period of rapid change, and remained responsive to prevailing social change movements as they grew older. On these grounds alone, one would expect older social workers in the sixties to have been less activist than their age-peers in the eighties.

Next consider the changing political environment with regard to the elderly in America. In the seventies and eighties, with their increasing numbers and life expectancy, older adults became "one of the most politically organized groups in the country" (Jones 1977:218–221). In addition, Weaver (1981:30–31) has argued that the effects of poverty and isolation have shaped the elderly into a coherent and self-conscious political force. Supporting his argument, he cites the rapidly rising membership rolls of such political interest groups as the American Association of Retired Persons (AARP) and the National Council of Senior Citizens.

Commenting, in the seventies, on the political power of mass membership associations such as AARP, Binstock (1974) described their formidable access to public officials through informal channels as well as through public platforms in the national media and in congressional hearings. In that same year, contrasting the political representation of the interests of the elderly with the experience of the past, Pratt (1974:106) remarked that the elderly of the seventies "have coalesced behind groups with a high level of political rationality and internal organizational discipline." Finally, the seventies witnessed a rapid growth of senior citizen centers and retirement communities throughout the country.

Along with the growth of political advocacy organizations and community supports, the elderly of the eighties voted in record numbers (*Statistical Abstract of the U.S.* 1988). As a result of such institutionalized efforts at political activism, the elderly are in a position to have their political interests taken more seriously than ever in our history.

Although the goals of the national "aging organizations" have not been "radical" nor their change strategies especially militant (Binstock 1981), the elderly have been involved in protest actions on the local level. These ad hoc protest groups have demonstrated their effectiveness in influencing such issues as reduced fares on public transportation and property tax relief (Jones 1977).

Whether through noninstitutionalized strategies or more socially accepted means, the elderly are making demands on society more than ever before with the recognition of their self-worth and the rejection of traditional stereotypes of their political impotence or indifference. This new political identity renders generalizations regarding aging and conservatism or aging and political "slow down" problematic if not obsolete.

The findings in this book should help to dispel any intramurally held notions that may exist about the greater conservatism and lesser activism of older social workers. Moreover, they suggest the possibility of putting the personal and historical experience, the organizational and technological knowledge, and the present political commitment of older social workers to work for social change.

RACIAL/RELIGIOUS GROUPS AND ACTIVISM

A third set of identities which are frequently associated with differences in political attitudes and behaviors are the racial/religious groups with which people identify. Members of such groups have their own political identities shaped by differences in their associated socioeconomic status, ethnic heritage, geographic concentration, historical experience, and orientations on public morality and social welfare (Lipset 1968).

In the sixties in the United States, race/religious identification was viewed as influential enough to have displaced loyalty to ethnic subcommunities (Herberg 1960). More recently, a Gallup poll found that a majority of

Americans (55%) rated religion as important in their own lives (Benson 1981:577).

In his classic book, *The Religious Factor,* Lenski (1961) categorized the major race/religious groupings in this country as White Protestants, White Catholics, Jews, and Blacks. Ranked in descending order by social acceptance these groups, he goes on to say, really constitute

> "status groups" in the sense in which Weber employed the term. That is to say, they are groups which are differentiated in terms of social honor, and where honor and respect are denied to a particular group, its members tend to react critically toward the social system as a whole, its key institutions, and their leaders (p. 157).

On the basis of this rank ordering, Lenski theorized that White Protestants and Catholics would be most desirous of maintaining the status quo and Jews and Blacks most critical of the system. In general support of his thesis, Lenski found that White Protestants and Catholics in the sixties were most conservative and Jews and Blacks most liberal on such social issues as racial integration, the welfare state, civil liberties, and foreign aid.

Substituting a measure of support for government-sponsored programs for Blacks in place of Lenski's measure of support for civil liberties, Nie, Verba, and Petrocik (1979:258) conducted a similar study in 1971.

Again, as with gender and age, comparison of findings from the two studies suggests that simplistic, ahistorical generalizations concerning the political effects of background characteristics across the decades are risky at best.

So, for example, in 1961 Lenski described White Protestants as relatively liberal on civil liberties and foreign aid, but conservative on racial integration and the welfare state. In the seventies, Nie and his associates found lower and middle class White Protestants to be generally more conservative on racial integration and government support programs for Blacks. However, by this time, upper class White Protestants had become more polarized into liberal and conservative camps on these issues.

In the early sixties, Lenski described White Catholics as "moderate" on welfare state issues, foreign aid, and civil liberties, but quite "conservative" on racial integration. In the early seventies, they were found by Nie, Verba, and Petrocik to be evenly divided between "liberals" and "conservatives" and spread across the ideological continuum on all of the issues.

Lenski found that Jews in the sixties were consistently "liberal" on all four issues, but most on the issue of racial integration. By the seventies,

Jews remained far more supportive than the general population of programs for Blacks and on foreign aid, but closer to the rest of the White population on the issue of racial integration.

Finally Blacks were described by Lenski in the sixties as "liberal" on racial integration and welfare state issues, but relatively "conservative" on civil liberties and foreign aid. Ten years later, they were found by Nie and associates to be the most "liberal" group in American society on all issues measured. This finding was sustained by research in the eighties (Cavanaugh 1985:4–8) which found Blacks most "liberal" on civil rights as well as on domestic and military spending.

Turning to political party identification, the findings are more consistent over the years. As did Lenski in the sixties, Nie, Verba, and Petrocik in the seventies found that White Protestants vote Republican more than the other race/religious groups; Catholics more Democratic than Protestants; Jews more Democratic than Protestants and Catholics; and Blacks most Democratic of all. Moreover, in a study of the elections in 1960, religious affiliation had a more powerful effect on party identification than occupation, education, and income (Knoke 1974).

Assessing Effects of Socio-Religious Identification

One would assume on the basis of the above discussion that racial/religious affiliation would be associated with significant differences in social worker activism in both of the studied eras. More specifically, in the sixties one would expect White Protestants and Catholic social workers to be least supportive and Jews and Blacks most supportive of activist goals and conflict strategies for social work. Likewise, it would be predicted that White Protestants and Catholics were least involved and Jews and Blacks most involved in noninstitutionalized forms of social action behaviors such as protest and civil disobedience.

For reasons that will be articulated below, predictions regarding institutionalized forms of social action behavior are more problematic in this context. Nevertheless, our brief review of the relevant political science research suggests that Blacks would score highest on this measure as well.

Making a prediction for the eighties is even more treacherous, particularly for White Protestants and Catholics. This is because these groups, or subgroups within them, were found by Nie, Verba, and Petrocik (1979) to have become more internally divided by the seventies with Catholics spanning the ideological continuum on all measures, while Jews were more liberal on government support for programs for Blacks but more conservative on racial integration.

In addition to the effects of the ideological shifts charted above, prediction is further complicated by the fact that there is no precise comparability between the measures of social work activism used in this study and the measures of ideological conservatism/liberalism employed in the studies previously cited. So, for example, although it is probably safe to assume that commitment to activist goals for social work is an indicator of a more "liberal" ideology, extrapolating from it to differences over government support for programs for Blacks versus racial integration or civil liberties (dimensions along which all four of the race/religious groups polarized or shifted) is impossible.

Finally, problems arise in extrapolating from measures of liberal/conservative ideology to some of our measures of activist behavior. Although it is probably safe to assume that for social workers participation in noninstitutionalized forms of activist behavior such as protest and civil disobedience is associated with ideological liberalism, links to the other measures of activist behavior are more problematic.

More specifically, are socially approved efforts by social workers to influence society, the outcome of an election, or the professionalization of social work associated with ideological liberalism or conservatism? In principle, they are neither. In practice, we do not know. (This conundrum reinforces our decision to refer to the foregoing behaviors as indices of "activism," per se, without reference to their ideological content.)

Given the formidable problems of shifting ideologies and noncomparability of measures described above, our "best" guesstimate for the eighties would be that Jews would have been relatively less activist on goals and conflict strategies than they were in the sixties and less likely to participate in noninstitutionalized forms of social action behavior. On the other hand, we would predict that Blacks in the eighties would continue to be the most activist social workers on all measures of attitudinal and behavioral activism.

Table 2.5 shows the proportion of White Protestant, White Catholic, Jewish, and Black social workers in 1968 and 1984 scoring high on each measure of social work activism. To begin with, we should note that although the proportion of White Catholics was just about the same in each sample (22% in 1968 and 25% in 1984), the relative proportions of White Protestants and Jews were quite different. Thus, 21 percent of the sample was made up of White Protestants in 1968 as compared with 48 percent in 1984. As for Jews, the corresponding proportions were 44 percent and 22

TABLE 2.5. Percent Scoring High on Social Activism by Religious Group Identification in 1968 and 1984

Measures of Activism	1968				1984			
	White Protestants	White Catholics	Jews	Black Protestants/ Catholics	White Protestants	White Catholics	Jews	Black Protestants/ Catholics
Activist Goals	24%	21%	29%	28%	35%[a]	45%[a]	30%[a]	55%[a]
Public Welfare Conflict Approval	44[c]	24[c]	46[c]	39[c]	44	54	48	40
Institutionalized Social Action Behavior[b]	50	42	45	64	88	83	79	90
Noninstitutionalized Social Action Behavior	21[c]	15[c]	37[c]	35[c]	14	13	22	23
Electoral Social Action Behavior	—	—	—	—	32[a]	32[a]	47[a]	53[a]
Professional Social Action Behavior	—	—	—	—	48	38	40	57
N =	172	181	368	109	276	142	126	35

a. p<.05.
b. p<.01.
c. p<.001.

percent respectively. Finally, 13 percent of the 1968 sample was Black as compared to 6 percent in 1984.[2]

These differences in racial-religious affiliation in our two samples are likely to be more a consequence of different sampling strategies and regional differences than of historical shifts in the racial-religious composition of social work. Hence, it must be remembered that the 1968 sampling was taken from New York City. The 1984 survey was based on a national sampling. The distributions of racial-religious groups in our two samples are disparate and offer different pictures of the racial-religious profile of social workers. Nevertheless, we would argue that analyses conducted within the samples, and within groups across the samples, remain valid.

Despite the sampling differences, in 1968 we find that in support of our prediction, White Protestant and Catholic social workers were least likely to endorse activist goals (24% and 21% respectively) and Jews and Blacks most activist on goals for social work (29% and 28% respectively). These differences are not statistically significant however.

Statistically significant differences ($p < .001$) are found on approval of conflict strategies in public welfare reform, although these findings only partially support our prediction. Here we see White Catholics least approving of conflict strategies (24%) and Jews most (46%). Surprisingly, however, Blacks score lower on this measure (39%) than do White Protestants (44%).

Turning to activist behaviors, in full support of our prediction, White Protestants and Catholics were least likely to be involved in protest in 1968 (21% and 15% respectively) and Jews and Blacks most involved (37% and 35% respectively). (These differences are significant at the .001 level.)

Finally, and in support of our prediction, for institutionalized forms of activist behavior we find that Blacks are most activist (64%). Moreover, on this measure, White Protestants score next highest (50%), followed by Jews (45%) and White Catholics (42%). (These differences are significant at the .01 level.)

In 1984, in support of our predictions, we see that Blacks are most activist in their commitment to activist goals for social work (55%) whereas Jews have moved from the highest score on this dimension in 1968 to the lowest in 1984 (30%). (These differences are significant at the .05 level.)

In addition, direct comparison within racial/religious categories in the 1984 and the 1968 samples indicates that whereas virtually the same proportion of Jewish social workers supported activist goals in the eighties as in the sixties (+1%), Blacks increased their support the most (27%).

White Catholics and Protestants also made sizeable increases on this dimension (+24% and +11% respectively). The differences were statistically significant for all groups ($p < .01$) except Jewish social workers.

On our measure of public welfare conflict approval, we find a pattern that departs dramatically from the one described above and from our prediction. Here Blacks are lowest in their support of conflict strategies for changing the welfare system (40%) and White Catholics are highest (54%). (These differences do not achieve a level of statistical significance, however.) And while Blacks, Jews, and White Protestants remain at virtually the same levels as in the sixties, White Catholics have moved from lowest to highest on this dimension (30%). (The difference is statistically significant at the .001 level.)

As for involvement in protest-type social action behaviors, in 1984 we find a pattern similar to the sixties with Blacks and Jews most activist (23% and 22% respectively) and White Protestants and Catholics least (14% and 13% respectively). (These differences are not statistically significant, however.) Nevertheless, it is noteworthy that Jews declined most from the sixties to the eighties on this measure (-15%) with Blacks close behind (-12%). (The difference was statistically significant for Jews, but not for Blacks.)

Finally on our three measures of socially approved forms of social action behavior Blacks are, as predicted, most activist. The differences between Blacks and other groups are statistically significant for the more general measure of institutionalized social action behavior ($p < .01$) and for electoral activism ($p < .05$). On the former measure, White Protestants are closest to Blacks (88% and 90%, respectively) and White Catholics and Jews are similar (83% and 79%, respectively). On the latter, Blacks and Jews remain quite similar (53% and 47%, respectively) and White Protestants and Catholics are equally low (32%). The differences approach statistical significance for profession-oriented social action behavior ($p < .06$). White Protestants are closest to Blacks (48% and 57%, respectively).

Let us try to summarize these complex patterns. In brief, our findings on the social action effects of racial/religious affiliation in the sixties versus the eighties are as follows:

(1). White Protestants remain relatively low in their activism with the exception of participation in institutionalized activism and efforts to enhance the professionalization of social work;

(2). White Catholics show striking increases in their commitment to activist attitudes and institutionalized social action behavior, but remain relatively low in other types of activist behavior, such as protest;

(3). Jews appear to be decreasing in their commitments to militancy although they maintain a relatively high level of involvement in electoral politics and increased their institutionalized activism;

(4). Blacks appear to be sustaining and possibly to some degree increasing in their relatively high level of activism, especially through efforts at institutionalized activism, professionalization, and electoral politics but remain least enthusiastic about the use of conflict strategies to bring about social welfare reform and are less involved in protest.

These generalizations are, for the most part, sustained when specialization, career status, and years in the field are controlled. The one exception has to do with involvement in profession-oriented social action behaviors. On that measure, the differences between the racial/religious groups diminish when these statistical controls are applied.

This could be a consequence of a higher concentration of Blacks locked into direct service positions after long years of service seeking a more collective route to mobility. It could also result from a relatively high concentration of White Protestant men occupying administrative positions in social work agencies. By virtue of their positions, they are routinely expected to take part in lobbying activity. While the social forces and personal motives that bring these two groups to profession-oriented activism are quite different, their goals remain the same, i.e., the protection and enhancement of social work professionalization.

Since we have promised the reader that we would be writing close to the data, we should point out that the foregoing discussion is speculative and warrants further research. Whatever the explanation, our findings suggest that differential career experiences of racial-religious groups may be linked to differences in involvement in profession-oriented activism.

The findings concerning White Catholics are not inconsistent with the work of Nie, Verba, and Petrocik (1979) cited earlier in this chapter. Their study described the Catholic community in the United States as becoming increasingly ideologically polarized. In this context, it is quite conceivable that those in social work represent the most ideologically liberal wing of that community. The fact that these social workers remain relatively low in their participation in most types of activism suggests that they have not as yet found acceptable channels for their ideological activism or that their commitments to activism are primarily attitudinal, and thus relatively shallow. Time and future research will answer that question as well.

Also consistent with the work of Nie, Verba, and Petrocik is the finding of the decreasing militancy and increasing institutional and electoral activism among Jews in social work. Despite their radical activist traditions and historic involvement in left-liberal movements (Isaacs 1974; Nie, Verba, and Petrocik 1979; Rubinstein 1982), over the last two decades Jews have become increasingly assimilated into American society and integrated into the political party structure (Milbrath 1965; Isaacs 1974; Rubinstein 1982).

In addition, the last twenty years has witnessed increasing tensions between Jews and Blacks (Syrkin 1980:278; Steele 1988). As a result, Jews in social work and in the rest of society appear to have withdrawn some of their personal and political investment in social change in behalf of the poor and in protest. Correlatively, they have increased their involvement in electoral politics.

For Blacks within social work, the maintenance of a relatively high level of activism and professional involvement may be a reflection of the traditionally high rates of participation among Blacks in voluntary associations (Babchuk and Thompson 1962; Hyman and Wright 1971) as well as their failure to be fully integrated into mainstream political, economic, and social structures. Research has shown that Blacks, especially Black women, are more likely to join and be actively involved in voluntary organizations than are Whites with the same social and demographic characteristics (Klobus-Edwards, Edwards, and Klemmock 1978; Antunes and Gortz 1975).

Moreover, the greater attitudinal commitment of Black social workers to social change in behalf of the poor and their relatively high involvement in protest is not surprising in view of the historic involvement of Blacks in the struggle for civil rights (Farley 1984) and the amount of poverty, joblessness, poor housing, inadequate health services, drugs, and other problems in low-income, Black communities.

In 1974, Eisinger showed that Blacks generally viewed protest more favorably than Whites. Subsequently, Isaac, Mutran, and Stryker (1980:209) developed a model to explain racial differences in the formation of political orientations based on 1969 survey data. The results indicate that for Whites integration into the system leads to avoidance of political means which threaten the system. Blacks, on the other hand, even those who are relatively integrated into the system, continue to perceive themselves as "underdogs in the system," and maintain an identification with the interests of less fortunate Blacks. As a result, they tend to maintain liberal to radical political orientations as well. Nevertheless, when compared with the sixties, Black social workers in the eighties are quite similar to Jews in their diminished involvement in protest and civil disobedience.

In addition, the high rate of involvement of Black social workers in electoral politics reflects a new societal trend for Blacks. Voting studies until the sixties consistently showed that Blacks participated in politics at a much lower rate than Whites (Milbrath 1965). By the early seventies, there had been a major increase in the voting turnout of Blacks and, thus, the difference between the social groups had declined (Nie, Verba, and Petrocik 1979).

By the eighties, spurred on by the insensitivity of the Reagan Administration, voter registration drives and the attraction of Jesse Jackson's campaigns for the Presidency, Blacks surpassed Whites in their relative degree of involvement in electoral politics. So, for example, a survey in 1984 conducted for *USA Today* found that 62 percent of Blacks, as opposed to 44 percent of Whites, said they had increased their interest in politics since 1980. And, during the first four years of the Reagan Administration the Census Bureau reported a sizeable increase in Black registration and voting turnout (Cavanaugh 1985).

Finally, the increasing effectiveness of the two Jackson Presidential campaign efforts suggests that electoral politics has become a new arena for grass-roots involvement by Blacks (Bush 1984). Although electoral activism is more socially accepted than protest, Jennings (1984) argues that the goal of this more institutionalized and less abrasive form of political behavior is still the dismantling of the White power structure and fundamental change in the distribution of wealth in American society.

More generally, racial and ethno-religious community identification has been viewed by political theorists as offering an alternative base of security and springboard to achievement, often through political activism, for those members without full access to opportunities provided by the dominant culture (Thomson and Knoke 1980). However, the erosion of the historic ties between Jewish and Black activists raises questions about the continuing applicability of the theory that holds that members of minority groups who share a mutuality of interests and are the targets of discrimination will be inclined to join together in their activism (Syrkin 1980; Steele 1988). Possibly, these two groups who historically have been committed to working together for social justice can link arms again within the arena of electoral politics.

Returning to Black social workers, despite their identification with less fortunate Blacks and their commitment to activist goals of changing the system on behalf of the poor, these social workers (as with any other group) are not immune from the politics of self-interest and job protection. This appears to be true even when their clients or Black "paraprofessionals" might benefit from what they oppose.

Hence, the 1984 finding that Black social workers are least supportive of protest strategies designed to achieve public welfare reform may be related to the fact that Black social workers are more likely than their White colleagues to be employed in the public welfare system. In the 1968 sample, 40 percent of the Black respondents were employed in public welfare and related governmental agencies as compared with 19 percent of Whites. By 1984, the corresponding figures had dropped precipitously to 7 percent of the Black respondents and 2 percent of the Whites. This suggests that Black social workers have suffered more from the cuts than their White colleagues (a drop of 33% versus 17% respectively). Nevertheless, they remained more than three times as likely to continue working in these programs than Whites.

Next to the poor themselves, it is very likely that Black social workers suffered most from the Reagan assault on the welfare system and from declassification efforts. The high level of effort by Black social workers in 1984 in behalf of social work licensing and against declassification may reflect this experience and related job insecurity. In this context, Black social workers may be less inclined to make the public welfare system a target of protest than Whites.

Conclusions

In a review of public opinion surveys from 1967 through 1975, Thomson and Knoke (1980) found that while the levels of socioreligious identification influenced political behavior, the pattern varied considerably over the years. Likewise, the empirical findings in this study suggest the following:

(1). the activism of social workers is determined, in part, by the racial-religious groups with which they identify;

(2). the influence of racial-religious group identification on social worker activism varies historically and generally parallels the political influence of the group on its members outside of social work;

(3). the influence of racial-religious group identification on social worker activism is significantly affected by the organizational and career experiences of the group within social work.

Future survey researchers, social work historians, and political organizers alike should keep these propositions in mind.

POLITICAL PARTY AFFILIATION AND SOCIAL WORK ACTIVISM

As with gender, age, and racial-religious roles and identities, political party affiliation and related ideologies often are firmly established long before individuals embark on their careers. This takes place through a complex pattern of direct and indirect primary group socialization (Hyman 1959). To reduce the potential impact of these already established political commitments, society has established professional norms of neutrality, organizational rules against intramural political campaigning, and public laws such as the Hatch Act.

Irrespective of societal efforts to mitigate the effects of political party affiliation and related ideologies from the work site, Dawson and Prewitt (1969:56) correctly remind us that political party identification "serves as an important reference point for the citizen's conceptual organization of the political world." And while norms against discussion of politics may support the notion that party affiliations and political beliefs have little to do with decisions about one's work, they are probably more influential than we would like to think.

In the context of social work activism, it would be hard to imagine that political party affiliation could not influence social workers' conceptions of goals for social work and appropriate means for achieving these goals. However (at least in the research literature), occupational norms concerning political neutrality within social work have effectively obviated consideration of this influence. As a result, political party affiliation, even more than gender, age, or racial-religious identification remains a "latent role" (Gouldner 1958), the influence of which has been heretofore uncharted.

In this section, we turn to the following questions:

(1). What are the political party affiliations of social workers? Have the political party affiliations of social workers changed from the sixties to the eighties?

(2). During these two periods, how did their party affiliations influence social workers' endorsement of activist goals and conflict strategies, and their participation in various forms of activist behavior?

Although these questions have never been systematically studied within social work, Spaulding, Turner, and McClintock (1963) surveyed the party affiliations of academically affiliated social scientists in 1960. They found that 10 percent of their 298 respondents classified themselves as Republicans, 78 percent as Democrats, 9 percent as Independents, and 3 percent refused to classify themselves (276). Spaulding, Hetrick, and Turner (1973) found a similar distribution of responses in 1970. (To our knowledge Spaulding and his associates did not explore the relationships between party affiliation and theoretical orientations, research interests, teaching content and style, and the like. Apparently, the influence of party affiliation is as much a taboo topic among social scientists as it is among social workers.)

While the occupational influence of party affiliation has gone unexplored, the differences between the two major political parties and the opposing social philosophies they espouse have been discussed by politicians ad nauseam. Needless to say, the Republican Party has long been associated with the spirit of capitalism and the ideals of "free enterprise." It is seen as supportive of business interests and opposed to labor unions. It is generally considered the "party of the status quo"—that is, if the status quo is politically conservative.

The Democratic Party, on the other hand, has long been associated with the left-liberal principles of the "welfare state" and is seen as supportive of labor unions. It is viewed as the "party of change."

In his classic survey in Detroit, Lenski's (1961: 121) respondents indicated that the Republican Party stood for "the rich and upper classes, free enterprise, and for conservatism." Alternatively, they said the Democratic Party stood for "the little man, for labor, for liberalism, and for more federal control."

Nie, Verba, and Petrocik (1979) measured the liberalism/conservatism of Republicans and Democrats in 1972 with regard to attitudes about the issues of racial integration, government action to benefit Blacks, welfare state programs, and foreign aid. Not surprisingly, they found major differences between the parties in that most of the Democrats were "liberals" and most of the Republicans were "conservatives." However, the Democrats tended to be more divided internally than the Republicans and the proportion of Democrats who were "conservative" had increased from previous years. The Republicans as well had moved further to the right in their attitudes.

Assessing Effects of Political
Party Affiliation

Since social workers are generally assumed to be left-liberal in their political attitudes and beliefs, one would predict that most social workers would be identified with the Democratic Party or with left-wing alternatives to it. In 1968, and in support of this expectation, when asked which political category described them best, 9 percent of the respondents identified themselves as Republicans, 73 percent as Democrats, 11 percent as having "no partisan identification" and 7 percent identified with a left-wing alternative party or ideology , e.g., Socialist Labor Party or Socialist.

The findings on social workers' political party affiliations in 1984 were quite similar to those in 1968. In our eighties sample, 9 percent were Republicans, 77 percent Democrats, 10 percent were not identified with any party or ideology and 4 percent had left-wing commitments outside the Democratic Party.

Since the Democratic Party traditionally has been identified with support of an increased governmental role in the economy and commitment to welfare state programs, it is hardly surprising that social workers are more highly affiliated with that party. Because of the left-liberal historic tradition in social work and because many social workers' current livelihoods and future opportunities depend on governmental support for social welfare programs it makes sense.

What is noteworthy, however, is the remarkably similar profile of political affiliation in the sixties and in the eighties. This suggests a very high level of ideological stability over the years. As such it runs counter to concerns sometimes expressed that the field is attracting much more politically "conservative" individuals and suggests, instead, that the recruitment base for social work has remained quite constant. In addition, these almost identical findings support our claims that the 1968 and 1984 samples are comparable.

Finally, it is interesting that the political affiliations of social workers in the sixties and eighties are so like the affiliations of academic social scientists [see our earlier discussion of the studies by Spaulding, Hetrick, and Turner (1973) and Spaulding, Turner, and McClintock (1963)]. Notwithstanding occasional attacks by social scientists that social workers are "muddle-headed do-gooders" or the returned salvos regarding "ivory towered academics," social workers and social scientists appear to be quite similar politically.

In comparison with the social action effects of racial-religious identification and age, predictions with regard to political affiliations are very straightforward. In this context, we would predict that social workers in the sixties and in the eighties who are affiliated with the Republican Party would be least supportive of activist goals, least approving of conflict strategies for public welfare reform, and least likely to participate in protest. Democrats, we would assume, would be more activist than Republicans on these measures and those identified with left-wing parties or ideologies most activist.

The position of "independents" on the foregoing measures of activism is harder to predict. On the one hand, "no partisan identification" could signify an ideology that emphasizes neutrality and/or noninvolvement in political and social action. Under these circumstances, one would predict low activism on these measures. Alternatively, it could signify a "radical" rejection of the institutionalized two-party system and be associated with relatively high endorsement of activist goals, conflict strategies, and protest.

As for institutionalized forms of social action behavior, we would predict that Republicans would be least activist because their political attitudes and beliefs and the behavioral manifestations of these attitudes and beliefs would probably receive little reinforcement from their social work colleagues. Democrats are likely to be more activist than Republicans on these measures.

For the reasons cited earlier, it is more difficult to predict the place of "independents." If their nonpartisanship indicates a preference for noninvolvement in social and political action and a conscious decision to reject political parties (Nie, Verba, and Petrocik 1979), one would assume low activism scores on each of these measures coupled with low endorsement of activist goals and conflict strategies and low involvement in protest. If "no partisan identification" represents a "radical" rejection of the two-party system and institutionalized channels, one would predict low scores on the first three measures and high scores on the last three. For those who affiliate with a left-wing party or ideology, prediction is equally difficult with regard to institutionalized forms of activism. These individuals might, to the extent that they reject all institutionalized political channels, score low on the three measures of institutionalized activism but high on activist goals, conflict strategies, and protest. Another possibility is that they would accept social work efforts at social change but reject electoral channels, scoring high on the former and low on the latter. Or, they may reject or endorse licensing and lobbying efforts in behalf of social work, depending on their ideological stance with regard to professionalization and/or declassification. Finally, they may be "across the board" activists who embrace all means for achieving social and political change.

Overall, despite relatively minor fluctuations in political party ideology and action, we would predict that the relationships between political affiliation and activism would remain constant between the sixties and eighties.

Table 2.6 indicates the percentage of social workers in 1968 and 1984 scoring high on social activism measures by political affiliation. In support of our prediction, we see that in 1968 20 percent of the Republicans, 23 percent of the Democrats, and 52 percent of those with left-wing affiliations endorsed activist goals for social work. In 1984, 16 percent of the Republicans, 38 percent of the Democrats, and 83 percent of those with left-wing affiliations were committed to activist goals for social work. (Both sets of relationships are statistically significant at the .001 level.)

The relative position of "nonpartisans" vis à vis Democrats has shifted from slightly more activist in the sixties to less activist in the eighties. For example, in 1968 nonpartisans were more likely to be active in protests than Democrats (31% vs. 27%). In 1984, Democrats were more active than nonpartisans (16% vs. 13%). The difference may reflect the changes that occurred in those who identified themselves as nonpartisans in the 1980s. The proportion of those who strongly identified with a major political party has been decreasing, and the proportion of nonpartisans has been increasing. By 1976, only about one out of four Americans could be considered a strong partisan while 37 percent were nonpartisans. Many of the nonpartisans were young, under 35, and appeared to have become nonpartisans because of a conscious decision to reject the parties (Nie, Verba, and Petrocik 1979). It may indicate a preference for noninvolvement in social and political action.

It may be that nonpartisans as a group are less committed to activism than Democrats because they consist of equal numbers of conservatives and liberals whereas Democrats are predominantly liberal. Nie, Verba, and Petrocik (1979:330–334) analyzed the results of a mock election in which McGovern was running against Goldwater. They reported that McGovern received over two-thirds of the Democratic votes; Goldwater received two-

TABLE 2.6. Percent Scoring High on Social Activism by Political Affiliation in 1968 and 1984

Measures of Activism	1968				1984			
	Republican	Democrat	Non-Partisan	Left-Wing Alternative	Republican	Democrat	Non-Partisan	Left-Wing Alternative
Activist Goals[b]	20%	23%	28%	52%	16%	38%	36%	83%
Public Welfare Conflict Approval[b]	22	39	32	77	17	50	41	79
Institutionalized Social Action Behavior	45	46	50	62	90[a]	85[a]	83[a]	75[a]
Noninstitutionalized Social Action Behavior[b]	12	27	31	66	7	16	13	62
Electoral Social Action Behavior[b]	—	—	—	—	18	38	21	65
Professional Social Action Behavior	—	—	—	—	47	46	32	50
N =	78	649	100	65	58	526	71	24

a. $p < .01$.
b. $p < .001$.

thirds of the Republican votes; and the nonpartisans split their votes fairly evenly.

The general picture also suggests a polarization on the issue of goals for social work. Thus, in 1968, the difference between Republicans and those with left-wing affiliations was 32 percent. In 1984 it was 67 percent, with Republicans declining 4 percent since the sixties and those on the left increasing by 31 percent.

A similar picture emerges when we look at political affiliation and endorsement of conflict strategies in public welfare reform. (Both relationships are statistically significant at the .001 level.) Here, however, the polarization of political groups is evident but less extreme in 1984 (55% in 1968 to 62% in 1984). This is perhaps because the differences between Republicans and those on the left were already quite sizeable in the sixties.

Looking at participation in protest and other forms of noninstitutionalized social action behaviors we find that political affiliation had a significant impact in the direction predicted both in 1968 and in 1984 ($p < .001$). However, on this measure polarization had not occurred over the years and every group had declined somewhat in its involvement in protest and civil disobedience.

Turning to institutionalized social action behavior (e.g., visit a public official, help in a fund-raising campaign), we find that in 1968 Republicans were least activist (45%) and those with left-wing affiliations were most activist (62%), although these differences are not statistically significant. In 1984, they were however ($p < .01$) and we find a reversal. Republicans were most activist (90%) and those on the left were the least activist (75%). All four groups, Republicans, Democrats, nonpartisans, and those with left-wing affiliations had markedly increased their institutionalized activism ($p < .01$). For example, Republicans increased by 45 percent and Socialists by 13 percent. Republicans had the most room to increase and those on the left were already quite active in the sixties.

Although "nonpartisans" in the eighties, were least involved in licensing and lobbying (32%) and those with left-wing affiliations and ideologies most involved (50%), these differences are not statistically significant. And because we have no comparable data for the sixties no historical differences can examined.

Most interesting here, however, are the similarities between Republicans, Democrats, and those with left-wing affiliations. These three groups were virtually equal in their involvement (47%, 46%, and 50% respectively) on this measure. This suggests that social action in support of social work professionalization transcends differences of political party preference and ideology.

Finally our 1984 data on electoral activism show that Republican social workers were least activist in election campaigns (18%), "nonpartisans" next (21%), Democrats next (38%), and those affiliated with the left most activist (65%). (These differences are statistically significant at the .001 level.)

This last finding, coupled with those above, strongly support the generalization that the relatively small group of social workers who define themselves as left of the Democratic Party, affiliate with left-wing organizations, and identify with left-wing ideologies are likely to express their activism through every available channel. By contrast, "nonpartisans" are generally low in their activism whatever the means of expression.

Conclusions

The findings with regard to political affiliation indicate that the political commitments that individuals bring to social work powerfully effect their involvement in social and political activism. And, while the political affiliations of social workers have remained remarkably constant between the sixties and the eighties, the effects of these affiliations have to some extent intensified.

This is particularly true with regard to conceptions of social work goals. Consequently, in the eighties even more than in the sixties, their outside political commitments influence the extent to which social workers embrace the idea that social change in behalf of the poor should be their priority.

Our overall findings in this section also suggest that in the sixties as well as in the eighties, the major differences in degree of commitment to social activism were between social workers who identified with a left-wing alternative party or ideology and all others. Nevertheless, the former have remained, over the past two decades, a relatively small minority within social work.

Consequently, on the basis of political affiliations of rank-and-file social workers alone, in the absence of an external left-liberal political movement, the prospects for social work being transformed into a "radical" institution appear limited.

SUMMARY

In this chapter we investigated the social action effects of the background characteristics and latent social identities which social workers bring to their careers. These variables are frequently disregarded in the social work literature or in informal discourse as explanations of attitudinal and behavioral differences in activism among social workers.

Four sets of demographic/social characteristics—gender, age, racial-religious identification, and political affiliation—were analyzed for their effects on social activism. All these characteristics were found to have a significant impact on social workers' social action attitudes and behaviors in the sixties. Males were more activist than females; younger social workers were more activist than older social workers in noninstitutionalized ways and less activist in institutionalized ways; Blacks and Jews were more activist than other racial-religious groups; and, finally, social workers identified with a left-wing party or ideology were more activist than Republicans, Democrats, and those without partisan identifications.

In the eighties, some of the foregoing characteristics had a lesser effect and some greater. Gender became less significant as did age. Thus, only in efforts oriented to increasing the professionalization of social work were males more activist than females. On all other measures women social workers were as activist, if not more so, than men.

In contrast to the sixties, age in the eighties was no longer associated with decreased militancy. Moreover, it was positively associated with involvement in institutionalized forms of activism.

For the majority of types of social activism, racial-religious group membership was less important in the eighties than it was in the sixties. Nevertheless, with the exception of the endorsement of conflict strategies in public welfare reform, Black social workers maintained relatively high levels of activism in the eighties as in the sixties. Jews, on the other hand, declined in their militancy. In the eighties, compared with White Protestants and Catholics, both Blacks and Jews were more active in electoral politics.

Finally, in the eighties, external political affiliations increased their influence on social workers' endorsement of activist goals, conflict strategies, and involvement in institutionalized forms of social action behaviors.

These findings highlight the influence that background characteristics and latent roles have on social worker activism. Second, the highly complex and differentiated patterns of influence by group and by type of activism reinforce the wisdom of having measures of activism that distinguish within and between attitudes and behaviors. Finally, they underscore the role of historical movements such as the women's movement, the political mobilization of the elderly, and the civil rights movement on social workers' social action attitudes and behaviors.

In the next chapter we consider the relative degree of professionalization of social workers in 1968 and in 1984 and compare social workers on this dimension with other occupational groups.

3

The Professional Attributes of Social Workers: The Sixties Versus the Eighties

From its beginnings as a self-conscious occupational group, social work has struggled with the question of whether or not it is a "true profession." As far back as 1915, the National Conference of Charities and Corrections engaged Abraham Flexner—a prominent scholar and consultant to the medical profession—to provide a definitive answer to this question. His report back to the Conference, entitled "Is Social Work A Profession?" (Flexner 1915) represented the first systematic and scholarly attempt to determine the professional status of social work.

Flexner began with a listing of attributes or traits that presumably separated professions from nonprofessions. Popple (1985:561) summarized Flexner's list. Flexner argued that professions distinguished themselves by the fact that they "engage in intellectual operations involving individual responsibility, derive their material from science and learning, work this material up to a practical end, apply it using techniques that are educationally communicable, are self-organized, and are motivated by altruism."

Next, he assessed the extent to which social work possessed these traits. His research strategy came to be widely used by occupational sociologists studying "established" and "would be" professions (Roth 1974). Known as the "attribute approach," it is based on what has come to be called the "trait model" of the professions (Forsyth and Danisiewicz 1985; Popple 1985).

As for the professional attributes of social workers, Flexner lauded them for being scientific, scholarly, and altruistic, and also found them in possession of a "professional self-consciousness." However, he concluded that the field was too broad in scope and too diffuse in its boundaries to be properly called a "profession" (Flexner 1915:585–588).

Since Flexner, social workers have pondered the Big Question again and again with historic regularity. In addition they have implemented numerous organizational strategies over the years as part of their collective "mobility project" to achieve professional status (Larson 1977). These have included: university affiliation for social work educational programs; accrediting systems for these programs; post-graduate certification systems; the development of a single professional association; a Code of Ethics; licensing legislation in several States, and so on.

At the same time, sociologists of the professions have continued to generate new listings of *differentia specifica* (Popple 1985:561) to separate professions from the mere aspirants to that status. Three score and ten years after Flexner, social scientists still had not achieved a consensus on these attributes or traits (Forsyth and Danisiewicz 1985).

In fact, some scholars have even challenged the appropriateness of the "trait model" for answering this question. In its stead, they have preferred a longitudinal variant of the trait model—the occupational "life history" approach (Caplow 1954; Wilensky 1964) or the "power model" (Friedson 1970; Johnson 1972; Larson 1977; Forsyth and Danisiewicz 1985). The former, attempts to identify the sequence of attributes that occupations must acquire over time in order to achieve the goal of professionalization. The latter determines the level of professionalization of a given occupation by the extent to which the occupation assumes a dominant position over its own division of labor, such that it gains control over the definition of its own work and over who has the right to do such work (Friedson 1970:xii).

Attempts to empirically test these two alternatives to the attribute approach have been less than successful, however. In the case of the "life history" model, Goode (1969) has shown that occupational histories vary so widely that the idea of a natural sequence of attributes is seriously questioned and adds nothing to the original "trait model."

In the case of the "power model," control over the division of labor may be a necessary condition of professionalization but it is hardly sufficient to claim professional status. So, for example, licensed electricians, plumbers, unionized stage hands, and other occupational groups that enjoy exclusivity of access to their work are rarely thought of as professionals. Moreover, a recent attempt by Forsyth and Danisiewicz (1985) to empirically test the validity of this approach looked very much like the kind of analysis one would conduct using the attribute approach. In their study, however, the key attribute is how workers in a given occupation perceive their autonomy, if any, from influence by the client and by the employing organization (p. 70).

Irrespective of their theoretical and methodological differences, what occupational sociologists have agreed upon is that the question has been asked incorrectly. Rather than asking whether a given occupation is a profession or not, they suggest that it makes more sense to view professionalization along a continuum from nonprofession to semiprofession to profession and to ask where on that continuum a given occupation can be located (Carr-Saunders 1965; Etzioni 1969; Toren 1972).

Unfortunately, however, consensus about how to pose the question has not led to a more definitive answer for social workers. Instead, disagreement about whether social work is a profession or not has simply evolved into disagreement concerning whether social work is a profession, a semiprofession, or none of the above.

In this debate, Greenwood (1957), Kadushin (1959), Cooper (1977) and Popple (1985) come down squarely in the "professional" camp. Carr-Saunders (1965), Etzioni (1969), and Toren (1972) opt for calling social work a "semi-profession." Finally, Epstein and Conrad (1978) and Wagner and Cohen (1978) have leaned in the direction of the understandably least popular "nonprofession" category.

Notwithstanding their disagreements, all of the authors cited above wrestle with the knotty question of social work professionalization by employing the attribute approach. Most do so, however, almost entirely on the basis of impressionistic data and their perceptions of and occupational aspirations for social work.

So, for example, Greenwood's article, entitled "Attributes of a Profession" (1957), lists five attributes that, for him, are indicators of an occupation's having achieved professional status. These are: possession of a systematic body of theory; community sanction; a culture; an ethical code; and allegiance to professional over bureaucratic authority.

Without quibbling over his selection of attributes, it should be pointed out that the degree to which social work manifests these qualities is subject to empirical research and validation. Greenwood does not engage in such a process. Instead, he justifies his claim that social work is a profession by simply asserting that the field possesses each of these traits, providing anecdotal evidence to support his position. Nevertheless, and for understandable reasons, Greenwood's is the most cited work on social work professionalization since Flexner and a model for the "sociological" claims to professionalization of several other occupations (Roth 1974).

Of all of the studies referred to above, only Popple (1985:573) approaches the issue of social work professionalization from a historical perspective. He concludes that what makes social work a profession is its "social assignment"—the "control of dependency in society," not exclusive possession of a body of knowledge and skills.

There were two studies based on empirical data. Wagner and Cohen (1978:29) interviewed social workers at three agencies in New York City about their working conditions to assess their professionalism. They concluded that social workers "have more in common with skilled workers than with physicians and lawyers." Finally, Epstein and Conrad's (1978) paper is singular in its extensive use of quantitative data to address the question. Although all these authors urge "deprofessionalization" of social work's conception of itself, they do so on the basis of research conducted at a single point in time. Because they do not have comparable data from the past or future, they cannot look at historical shifts in attributes of social work professionalization. As a result, they are left with a "half-empty/half-full" problem in assessing the level of professionalization. Moreover, they have no way of knowing whether the glass is being emptied or filled.

While neither in this chapter nor this entire study can we provide a definitive answer to the "Big Question" in the "is it, or isn't it?" form that was put before Flexner, nor can we precisely answer the question in its tripartite, revised version, we can attempt to do what no previous study has done: We shall try to address the professionalization question in a relatively objective manner, with quantitative data, in a historical context. Paraphrasing Vollmer and Mills (1966) we ask the question, "how professionalized, in certain identifiable and measurable respects, was social work in the sixties and in the eighties?"

More specifically, using generally agreed-upon professional attributes, we ask how respondents scored in 1968 along these dimensions. Next, after almost two decades of concerted effort by the National Association of Social Workers (NASW), the Council on Social Work Education (CSWE), and other social work organizations to increase the professionalization of social work, we ask whether social workers were any closer to the professional end of the continuum in 1984 than they were in 1968. Next, in a more limited fashion, we consider how social workers in the sixties and in the eighties compared to other occupational groups with regard to these traits. Finally, we consider differences in the attributes of professionalization by practice specialization and by auspice.

Because there is so much disagreement in the social work literature on the issue of professionalization, we approach the subject cautiously, without making any predictions. Instead, our intent is to simply ask the relevant questions and describe patterns of response in the two decades.

ASSESSING THE PROFESSIONAL ATTRIBUTES OF SOCIAL WORKERS

Those who have attempted to translate professional traits of social workers and other occupational groups into measurable terms have done so in numerous ways. Building on Goode's (1957) seminal paper on the professions as "communities within a community," they derive the following empirical measures of the extent to which:

- the community is represented in the worksite;
- the workers actively participate in this community outside of work;
- this community serves as a reference group for its members despite worksite pressures in the opposite direction;
- the workers maintain the ideal of service;
- the workers are committed to an ideology that supports professionalization;
- the workers maintain a sense of professional autonomy.

Organizational Professionalization

In some studies, measures and discussions of professionalization focus on the work environments in which people practice. In this context, "professionalization" may refer to the amount of training required to occupy particular positions within an agency or the proportion of people in those positions within the agency that have full training.

Etzioni comments, for example, that professional and semi-professional organizations can be distinguished by the "proportion of professionals" on their staffs. He suggests that "at least 50%" of the staff must have full professional training if the organization is to be classified as "professional" (1964:77–78).

Similarly, Vinter remarks that the way to professionalize the "organizational climate" of a social work agency is to introduce more professionally trained personnel (1959:250).

March and Simon speak of the professionalization of specific jobs, by which they mean the "specific formal training" required for these positions (1958:70). In their study of social workers, Hage and Aiken actually devise such a measure (1967).

To measure the degree of professionalization of the structures within which social workers in the sixties routinely practiced, respondents in 1968 were asked to indicate "the percent of the total number of employees in social work jobs" in their agency who had a graduate degree in social work. Those who responded that 100 percent of the social workers in their work setting had graduate degrees were scored "high" on "organizational professionalization." In order to assure comparability, respondents in 1984 were asked the same question and scored in the same way.

Table 3.1 shows the percentage of respondents in 1968 and in 1984 scoring high on professionalization of the work site. Using the graduate degree as our criterion of organizational professionalization, we find that 42 percent of those in the 1968 sample worked in settings in which 100 percent of the social workers had graduate degrees, but that number declined to 37 percent in 1984. (This difference is statistically significant at the .05 level.)

Interpreting the responses to this question relative to professionalization of the worksite in the sixties and in the eighties is difficult, however. In the years between the two surveys, CSWE began accrediting undergraduate social work programs while NASW opened its doors to BA degree social workers. As a consequence, those who were organizationally defined by

TABLE 3.1. Percentage in 1968 and 1984 Scoring High on Working in Agencies Peopled Predominantly by MSWs or by MSWs and BSWs

	1968	*1984*
Organizational Professionalization		
MSW[a]	42%	37
MSW and BSW	—	62
N =	826	624

a. $p < .05$.

CSWE and NASW as "nonprofessionals" in 1968 were considered "fully qualified professionals" in 1984.

Table 3.1 indicates the percentage of respondents in 1984 who worked in agencies in which 100 percent of the social workers had BSW degrees and/or graduate degrees in social work. Using the graduate degree and the BSW degree as the criteria of organizational professionalization, we find that 62 percent of those in the 1984 sample scored high on professionalization of the work site. This contrasts with 42 percent in 1968 who worked in settings in which 100 percent of the social workers had graduate degrees. We have no data on BSWs for the 1968 sample. (This difference is statistically significant at the .01 level.) Thus, to determine whether social workers should be considered more professionalized in their work settings in 1968 or 1984, it depends on which criteria are used.

This is an instance in which professionalization indicators based on the "trait model" conflict with those based on the "power model." Hence, by extending the definition of "professional education" to include undergraduate programs and by extending access to "professional positions" to those with undergraduate degrees in social work, CSWE and NASW have increased their organizational and individual power bases, the size of their memberships, and their financial resources. Consequently, social work has tighter control over its own division of labor and who has access to it (Leighninger 1978), and, by implication, more professional clout in the external society.

At the same time, this political strategy has reduced the skill and experience levels ideally associated with social work jobs. In so doing, social work has diminished the strength of its claim to professionalization on the basis of such attributes of expertise as education and experience.

The evidence as to whether social workers with a BSW degree are as professionalized as those with an MSW degree is limited, conflicting, and inconclusive. Posey (1978:43) and Hanna (1975:120–121) each found that graduate social workers had more professional attitudes than BSW social workers. Ward et al. (1985) found that social workers, regardless of their level of education, are not much different from one another in regard to such professional values as belief in service to the public, calling to the field, and autonomy. Cyrns (1977) discovered that baccalaureate social workers had a more positive orientation to clients than master's-level social workers.

The historical changes in social work have made it difficult to say whether the decline in the percentage of social workers with graduate degrees in social work positions represents a decline in the professionalization of the workplace or an effective strategic redefinition within social work of what is a "professional" (Leighninger 1978).

If the latter is true, a decline in the percentage with graduate degrees, coupled with an increase of those with undergraduate degrees, could mean greater rather than lesser professionalization of social work agencies. In the absence of additional data, we cannot say which of these interpretations is likely to be correct.

A simpler interpretation of the differences in organizational professionalization in the sixties and the eighties is that the bureaucratic declassification of social work jobs in public agencies and publicly supported private agencies lessened the proportion of positions controlled by social workers in the eighties.

Purchase of service contracting (POSC) may be another reason for the decline. Ghere (1981) found that the proportion of public agency staff with human services backgrounds decline as the level of POSC activity increases. Social worker positions lost are filled by those with management backgrounds. Between 1971 and 1978, the percentage of funding under the Social Security Act involving POSC increased from 25 percent to 54 percent (Mueller 1978, 1980). A more recent study indicated that the strength of this trend is increasing (Martin 1985).

The correct interpretation of our findings with regard to organizational professionalization must await further research. Nevertheless, the findings do indicate that this attribute of professionalization in social work is one that has been highly dynamic in the last two decades.

Professional Participation

A second set of attributes of professionalization which commonly appears in occupational studies refers to the extent to which people participate in the occupational community and culture outside of the worksite. In other words, how actively do they participate in professional associations, conferences, knowledge development, and the like?

Hage and Aiken (1967:508–509), for example, developed an index of the "extra-organizational professional activity" of social workers, based on the number of their professional association memberships, meetings attended, papers given, and high offices held in such professional associations. This composite index is seen as measuring the degree of "professional involvement" of their study participants.

In another study of social workers, Billingsley (1964 a, b) uses similar indicators as measures of the participation of respondents in the "professional subsystem."

The use of such measures is not confined, however, to studies of social workers. In a comparative study of university professors, lawyers, and engineers, Wilensky (1964:152–158), for example, uses readership of professional journals as a component item in his overall measure of these groups' "professional orientations."

To determine the extent of professional participation of social workers in 1968, respondents were asked questions taken from Billingsley's and Wilensky's questionnaires. These questions required information about participation in national and local NASW chapters, papers presented to professional groups, papers published, conferences attended, and readership of professional journals. The same questions were put to social workers in the 1984 sample. An identical scoring system based on the extent of professional participation on each of these dimensions was devised and applied to both samples (Epstein 1969:220). A score of "high" was given to those who were in the top third of the samples on all of these items combined.

How do social workers in the sixties and those in the eighties compare on their levels of professional participation? Table 3.2 provides the answer. Here again, the answer is complex.

Using our overall index of professional participation to compare social workers of the sixties with those of the eighties, we find that 32 percent of

TABLE 3.2. Percentage in 1968 and 1984 Scoring High on Professional Participation

Participation	*1968*	*1984*
Professional Participation Index	32%	36%
Papers Presented to Professional Group[a]	47	39
Published Articles in Professional Journals[a]	27	18
Participation in NASW at Local Level	10	9
Attended Social Work Conferences in Last Year	85	86
Thorough Reading of Social Work Journals[a]	5	12
N =	899	682

a. $p < .001$.

the former scored high on this measure as compared with 36 percent of the latter. This suggests a small, but statistically insignificant rise in professional participation.

A closer examination of responses to individual questions, however, reveals a number of statistically significant differences that are concealed in the combining of responses. So, although the relative extent of participation in NASW and professional conferences remains about the same, social workers in the sixties were significantly more likely than those in the eighties to present papers to a professional group (47% versus 39%, respectively) or to publish articles in professional journals (27% versus 18%, respectively). And, although social workers in the eighties were significantly more likely to "thoroughly" read their professional journals than their sixties' predecessors (12% versus 5%, respectively), an overwhelming majority (88%) of the respondents in 1984 gave their journals only a "partial reading" at best.

Together with the consistently high levels of conference attendance (between 85% and 86%), these findings may reflect a more passive, consumer orientation to professional participation and development of knowledge than in the sixties. Or, it may be that with the substantial increase in NASW membership and the relatively constant number of conferences and social work journals, there were relatively fewer opportunities for conference presentations and publication in the eighties than there were in the sixties. Finally, lower presentation and publication involvement may be a consequence of the lowered educational standards for entry into NASW.

Reeser compared the professional participation of respondents with a BSW degree in 1984 to those with a graduate or doctoral degree. She used the overall index of professional participation to compare these groups, but found no significant differences. There were also no significant differences in responses to individual items. Baccalaureate social workers were not less likely than graduate level social workers to participate in NASW chapters, to present or publish papers, to attend conferences, or to read professional journals. Thus, our findings on the decreased presentations and publications of social workers in the eighties do not seem to be explicable in terms of the decreased educational standards for entry into NASW. However, caution must be exercised in concluding that BSW social workers are as professionalized in their participation as graduate social workers. Research has indicated that baccalaureate social workers have a low level of affiliation with NASW (Mahler 1982; Ward et al. 1985). Thus, the BSWs who belong to NASW may not be representative of BSWs in general.

Whether our findings may be explained by the more general emphasis on consumerism that has been associated with the "yuppie movement," or today's relatively fewer opportunities for conference presentation and publication awaits further research.

Commitment to Professional Role Orientations

Without question the most frequently used measures of professional attributes are based on the concept of the "professional role orientation" or "reference group." In his aptly titled paper, "The Professionalization of Everyone?", attesting to the common usage of this construct, Wilensky (1964) remarks:

> Several observers of occupational life—in contexts as diverse as the Wisconsin civil service, the Office of Naval Research, big national labor unions, general hospitals in Missouri, a liberal arts college, and university social science departments—have independently come to very similar conclusions about the types of orientations professional and executive personnel have toward their work (orientations variously labeled "career commitments," "role concepts," "job identification," or "reference groups") (p. 150).

Studies that employ this set of ideas regard the professional role orientation as one of a number of alternative and potentially conflicting normative commitments around which careers may be organized. Which commitment takes priority depends on which of the total number of groups with which the worker interacts, constitutes his/her primary reference group. Thus, workers may identify most with, and want to be judged by, professional colleagues and leaders in the profession. Or, they may become "organizational people," committed to career mobility, with the primary concern being satisfying their supervisor and/or the agency administration. Another possibility is that they may give primary allegiance to the expressed desires of their clients, even when such consumer-oriented behavior involves a violation of professional or organizational values or norms.

The first normative pattern is generally thought of as most "professional." The second is variously labeled as an "agency" or "bureaucratic" or "careerist" orientation. The third is generally referred to as a "client" or "consumer" orientation.

Assessing Social Workers' Role Orientations. The role orientations of social workers have been explored in two previous studies: one by Billingsley (1964) of MSWs in child welfare and family counseling agencies; and the other by Scott (1965) of nondegreed workers employed in a public welfare agency. In addition, Wilensky (1964) found such measures useful in distinguishing the comparative role-orientation profiles of professors, lawyers, and engineers.

Although the theoretical constructs underlying them were very much the same, the measures and scoring systems used by each of the foregoing investigators differ. Scott, for example, measured professional role orientation by asking respondents to select and rank sources from which is received "the greater part of your intellectual and professional stimulation in connection with your work?" The response alternatives included internal agency sources such as "immediate supervisor" and "agency administration," and sources external to the agency such as "professional books and journals" and "professional people outside the agency." A high commitment to a professional role-orientation was indicated by selection of external professional sources of stimulation.

Billingsley's Role Orientation scale required respondents to choose between conflicting demands of collegial norms, client needs, agency policies, and pressures from community influentials. From responses to six questions in which the conflicting demands of pairs of "subsystems" were presented, an index of commitment to a professional orientation for each respondent could be computed.

Wilensky's Role Orientation index is the most complex of the three. On the basis of more "professionally oriented" responses to three questions — "Whose judgement should count most when your overall professional performance is assessed?"; "What are the sources of job satisfaction?"; and "How thoroughly do you read professional journals?"—a comparable measure for social workers could be constructed.

Each of the foregoing authors offers a distinct formula for assessing the strength of their respective respondents' professional role orientations. Incorporating these measures and scoring systems into his study, Epstein (1969:42–44,220) was able to measure the percentage of social workers in his 1968 sample scoring "high" on each measure. By doing the same, Reeser (1986) made it possible for us to compare social workers in the sixties with those in the eighties on this key attribute of professionalization. In addition, replication and administration of Wilensky's measure, made it possible for us to compare our respective data on social workers' role orientations with Wilensky's data on university professors, lawyers, and engineers.

Table 3.3 shows the percentage of respondents in 1968 and 1984 scoring high on the Scott, Billingsley, and Wilensky professional role orientation scales.

There was no significant difference found between the 1968 and 1984 samples on the Scott index. We consider Scott's Role Orientation index to be flawed because he scored stimulation from colleagues as a bureaucratic response. Colleagues are an internal source of stimulation but, in contrast to choosing one's supervisor or the agency director, they do not clearly represent primary loyalty to the organization. Billingsley employed choosing "agency policies" as a bureaucratic response in his index. This is a less ambiguous response than choosing colleagues or one's supervisor. Wilensky scored choosing colleagues in the agency as a professional response. Thus, we scored colleagues as a professional response in computing the Scott index for our samples.

Another problem with Scott's Professional Role Orientation index is that he developed it and tested it with nondegreed social workers in a less professionalized work setting (public welfare). For all these reasons, Scott's index will not be utilized to compare the professional attributes of practice groups in this chapter or to examine the relationship between professional attributes and social work activism in the next chapter.

On both the Billingsley and the Wilensky indices, a greater proportion of social workers in 1984 scored high on professional commitment than in 1968 (55% versus 31% and 25% versus 5%, respectively). (These differences were statistically significant at the .001 level of significance.)

TABLE 3.3. Percentage in 1968 and 1984 Scoring High on Professional Role Orientation

Role Orientation	1968	1984
Scott Professional Role Orientation	71%	73%
Billingsley Professional Role Orientation[a]	31	55
Wilensky Professional Role Orientation[a]	5	25
$N =$	833	682

a. $p < .001$.

These findings indicate that social workers in the eighties were significantly more professionalized in regard to their choice of a primary reference group than were their sixties predecessors.

More detailed comparisons of the responses to individual items by "professionally" trained social workers in the fifties, sixties, and eighties (Billingsley versus Epstein and Reeser) and by "professionally" trained social workers with university professors, lawyers and engineers (Epstein and Reeser versus Wilensky) are also instructive.

Table 3.4 (p. 84) shows the reference group preferences of respondents in Billingsley's (1964) study of master's degree caseworkers in a child and family treatment setting in comparison with our data from social workers in 1968 and in 1984. On the critical choice dimension of following one's "own professional judgement" versus "agency policies" there is continuous increase over the years in "professional orientation" (39% in 1957, 48% in 1968, and 56% in 1984) and a corresponding decrease in "bureaucratic orientation." (Since the Billingsley sample is drawn from two agencies rather than from NASW, the fifties, sixties and seventies samples are, strictly speaking, noncomparable. As a result, tests of statistical significance among the three samples were not computed. The differences between the 1968 and 1984 samples were statistically significant at the .001 level however.) These findings offer evidence of an increasing commitment to professional versus bureaucratic norms over the last four decades.

As for professional versus client commitments, the story is more ambiguous—theoretically, operationally, and empirically. In theory, there should be no conflict between a professional's definition of the client's "needs" and the professional's own judgment about what to do. This is consistent with many theoretical discussions dating back to Flexner which claim that professions are unique in that their service orientations link their own success and effectiveness with their clients' interests (Flexner 1915; Parsons 1939; Goode 1960; Wilensky 1964). According to these theoretical perspectives, there can be no conflict between the client's need and professional norms.

The problem confronts social workers and other occupational groups when the client's requests conflict with the worker's definitions of need. The Billingsley question is then operationally ambiguous because it doesn't reflect that distinction. Instead, it asks respondents whether they would endorse a social worker's meeting "the needs of clients," "even though a particular act is considered 'unprofessional' by colleagues."

In contrast with increasingly "professional" responses to the conflict between professional judgment and agency policies over the years, re-

TABLE 3.4. Percentage in 1957, 1968, and 1984 Choosing the Profession, Clients, or Agency in Conflict Situations

Role Orientation	*1957*	*1968*	*1984*
Follow Professional Judgment Even if Against Agency Policy	39%	48%[a]	56%[a]
Choose Professional Objections of Colleagues	43	31[a]	54[a]
Follow Professional Judgment Over What Community Thinks	98	97[a]	94[a]
N =	110	899	669

a. $p < .001$.

sponses to this problematic question concerning professional versus client commitment reveal a nonlinear pattern. Hence, in 1957, 43 percent of Billingsley's sample chose professional norms over client "need" as compared to 31 percent in 1968 and 54 percent in 1984. (The difference between the latter two samples is significant at the .001 level.)

It is possible that this apparent decline in professional commitment in the sixties is associated with an increased consumer or client advocacy orientation in the sixties as compared to the fifties. One would expect, therefore, for social workers to choose to respond to client "need" even if it led to accusations of "nonprofessional" behavior. This is not likely to explain the apparent increase in commitment to professional norms versus the client's definition of their needs in 1984, however. We say this because of data we have from social workers in the sixties and eighties samples. Both groups were asked whether they agreed that there was a "great difference between low-income clients' views of their problems and their real problems." In response to this question, fewer social workers in the eighties agreed than in the sixties (34% versus 22%, respectively). This finding, (significant at the .001 level), implies that social workers in the eighties were not more likely than those in the sixties to distinguish between their clients' definitions of need and their own. In fact, it was just the opposite.

Finally, with regard to professional commitments versus commitments to influential people in the community, the pattern is consistent, clear, and unambiguous. In this area of choice, well over 90 percent chose professional commitments in each sample over the last four decades. (The slight decline between 1968 and 1984 on this measure is statistically significant at the .001 level.)Returning to table 3.3, we see the percentage of social workers in 1968 and in 1984 scoring high on Wilensky's measures of professional role orientation. As with the Billingsley measure, we see that on the Wilensky index, social workers in the eighties had a significantly stronger orientation to the profession than did those in the sixties ($p <$ .001). For example, they were more likely to mention professional colleagues and leaders in social work as those whose judgement should count most regarding professional performance.[1]

Role Orientations of Professors, Lawyers, Engineers and Social Workers. Table 3.5 shows the percentage of social workers in 1968 and in 1984 and the percentage of professors, lawyers, and engineers from Wilensky's study that scored high on professional, careerist, and client orientations.[2] Without knowing whether or not the latter three occupational groups have changed since 1963 when the Wilensky data were collected, we see that in the sixties social workers were closest to engineers in their role orientation profiles. More specifically, both groups were relatively low in commitment to their respective professions, relatively high in commitment to their organizational careers, and moderate in their commitment to clients.

TABLE 3.5. Percent of Professors, Lawyers, Engineers, and Social Workers in 1968 and 1984 Scoring High on Wilensky Professional, Careerist, and Client Orientation Indices[a]

High On	*Professors*	*Lawyers*	*Engineers*	*Social Workers (1968)*	*Social Workers (1984)*
Professional Orientation	51%	25%	11%	5%	25%
Careerists Orientation	3	6	25	27	35
Client Orientation	30	51	35	37	47
N =	99	207	184	833	682

a. See Wilensky (1964: 153–154).

Since then, social workers have increased in their commitment to each of these dimensions with the greatest increase (20%) in commitment to the profession. (Because of the way in which the role orientation scores are computed, an increase on each dimension is mathematically possible only on the Wilensky scales. On the Scott and Billingsley scales, an increase on one dimension generally results in a decrease on the other.)

More generally, Table 3.5 suggests that each of the occupations presented have their own unique role-orientation profiles. However, these profiles may change historically. So, while social workers in the sixties were most like engineers, by the eighties they were very much like lawyers in their degree of professional commitment (second highest) and client commitment (highest). Nonetheless, eighties' social workers were also more committed to their bureaucratic careers than any of the other occupations studied.

This unique role orientation profile is consistent with Scott's (1965) description of social work as a "heteronomous profession" in which the demands of profession, organization, and client are more integrated and less conflictual than in other professions. If this is true, one would expect social workers to experience less role conflict than those professionals who are often conceived of as private practitioners (e.g., lawyers and doctors), but who are, in fact, organizationally employed. This question awaits future researchers.

The profile is also consistent with Wilson, Voth, and Hudson's (1980:28) finding in their study of social workers that bureaucratic and professional orientations are independent dimensions. Social workers were likely to value autonomy and innovation in their work at the same time as they valued bureaucratic elements.

Clearly, however, the role-orientation scores of social workers in the eighties show an increased level of professionalization when compared to those in the sixties. The changes since the sixties may be a consequence of conscious strategies to increase professionalization such as efforts to define a unique knowledge base and skill repertoire for social workers (Minahan 1981), the growth in size and organizational strengthening of their professional association (Beck 1977), licensing successes (NASW News 1985), and revision of the code of ethics (McCann and Cutler 1979).

Also awaiting future research is the question of whether social workers will continue to increase in their commitment to a professional reference group, and if so, why.

Commitment to the Ideology of Professionalism

In their book entitled *Professionalization,* Vollmer and Mills (1966: viii) make a distinction between "professionalization as a social process" and "professionalism as an ideology." Stressing the independence of these concepts, they remark:

> many occupational groups that express the ideology of professionalism in reality may not be very advanced in regard to professionalization. Professionalism may be a necessary constituent of professionalization, but professionalism is not a sufficient cause for the entire process of professionalization.

Our previously discussed measures of professionalization are essentially "social-structural" and as such are assumed to be reflections of the professionalization process. The ideology of professionalism, on the other hand, is built on a set of social-psychological attitudes, beliefs, and values which are presumed to be indirectly associated with the process of professionalization and directly associated with aspiration to professional status.

Following Vollmer and Mills, the content of this ideology, the extent of commitment to it, the degree to which this commitment has changed since the sixties, and the extent to which it is correlated with the process of professionalization remain open questions to be addressed through empirical research. In this section we focus on the first three questions. In the next chapter, we consider the last.

Not surprisingly, there is disagreement among theoreticians and empirical researchers about which attitudes, beliefs, and values are central to this ideology. Drawing from the writings of several authors, Epstein (1969) developed an original index of commitment to the ideology of social work professionalism on the basis of the degree to which respondents agreed with statements emphasizing political neutrality (Pray 1959; Heffernan 1964), professional decorum (Caplow 1954), control over one's emotions (Parsons 1958; Wilensky and Lebeaux 1965), and the superiority of worker versus client problem definitions (Greenwood 1957; Goode 1961; Galper 1975; Grønbjerg, Street, and Suttles 1978; Wilding 1982). In her 1984 study, Reeser constructed a similar index. However, the factor analysis she employed to choose her component items required that she substitute a single item about professional self-regulation (Hall 1968) for Epstein's item about professional definition of client need. In all other respects, Reeser and

Epstein's scales were identical. (For the component items, see Appendix B to this volume.) A score of "high" was given to those who were in the top third of the samples on all these items combined.

Table 3.6 shows the percentage of social workers in the sixties and those in the eighties who agree with each of the component statements associated with the ideology of professionalism.

Analysis of the responses of social workers in the sixties and in the eighties to these scales indicates no significant difference in commitment to the ideology of professionalism over the past two decades.

There were also no significant differences in response to most of the individual component items. Only approximately one third of the social

TABLE 3.6. Percentage in 1968 and 1984 Approving of Values of Professionalism

Values	1968	1984
Emotional Neutrality: Social Workers Should Have Strong Control Over Emotions[a]	68%	59%
Professional Superiority: Great Difference Between Low-Income Client's View of the Problem and the Real Problem[a,b]	34	22
Decorum: Social Workers Should Maintain A Restrained and Dignified Manner With Clients	31	35
Political Neutrality: Social Workers Should Avoid Public Expression of Political Values in Professional Roles	26	25
Political Neutrality: Social Workers Should Avoid Political Discussions With Clients	26	29
Professional Self Regulation: Persons Who Violate Professional Standards Should be Judged Only by Their Professional Peers[c]	—	56
$N =$	899	670

a. $p < .001$.
b. This item was not included in Reeser's index but was included in her questionnaire.
c. This item was not included in Epstein's index or his questionnaire.

workers in 1968 and 1984 believed in maintaining a restrained and dignified manner with clients (31% vs. 35%, respectively). Most social workers in 1968 and 1984 were committed to the public expression of political values in professional roles (26% vs. 25%, respectively) and in discussion with clients (26% vs. 29%, respectively). Over half of the social workers in 1984 believed in professional self-regulation.

There were, however, two significant differences that did emerge on individual items. Thus, table 3.6 shows that a greater proportion of social workers were committed to the exercise of strong emotional control in 1968 than in 1984 (68% versus 59%, respectively). In addition, there was a statistically significant decline from the sixties to the eighties in the percentage of social workers who believed that the workers' definitions of problems were superior to the definitions of low-income clients (34% versus 22%, respectively). (Both of these differences were significant at the .001 level.)

In other words, while social workers have significantly increased their commitment to their professional reference group since the sixties, their commitment to an ideology of professionalism has not. Few social workers in either era were committed to a majority of the dimensions. In fact, on two of the dimensions, professional superiority and emotional neutrality, professionalism has decreased significantly.

At the very least, these findings support Vollmer and Mills' (1966) contention that the process of professionalization and commitment to an ideology of professionalism are separate and distinct phenomena.

In addition, they contradict the commonly held belief that social workers have become more "professionalized" in their ideologies since the sixties and consequently less accepting of the problem definitions offered by the poor (Cloward and Epstein 1965). Though part of the folklore (Friedson 1973) of social work, these beliefs about social workers appear to be more myth than reality. Thus, any decrease in social work's commitment to the poor since the sixties is likely to have another explanation.

The question remains, however—what effect does commitment to the ideology of professionalism have on the social activism of individual social workers? In the following chapter we answer that question.

THE EXERCISE OF PROFESSIONAL AUTONOMY

The granting of autonomy and discretionary authority in the workplace and to an occupation as a whole is believed to be a significant and highly sought-after attribute of professions. The absence of professional autonomy, on the other hand, has been described as a major barrier to social work's becoming a "full-fledged" profession (see Toren 1972; Scott 1966; Wagner and Cohen 1978; Burghardt 1982).

Drawing his theoretical perspective from the work of Weber, Scott (1965) has argued that because social workers practice in "heteronomous" organizations the amount of autonomy granted to them is inevitably limited. Thus, according to Scott, in addition to being guided and controlled by professional norms and expert knowledge, social workers are appropriately and necessarily required to take their cues from administrative values and superiors in the organization.

It should be pointed out, however, that Scott's view of social work's potential for autonomous practice was limited in itself by the fact that he was generalizing from an agency that was low on the scale of organizational professionalization. In other words, by studying the practice norms of nondegreed social workers in a public welfare agency he was drawing conclusions about all of social work from a setting in which social workers are likely to be least autonomous.

By contrast, Wagner and Cohen (1978:41) studied the working conditions of three New York City agencies employing MSW social workers in the seventies. Despite the relatively high level of professional training in these organizations, the authors found as well that their sample populations experienced "severe limitations on their autonomy."

Some of the explanations given for social work's difficulty in acquiring greater autonomy in the work setting are its inability to demonstrate exclusive competence in a body of knowledge and skills (see Toren 1976; Wilensky 1964; Simon 1977); lack of power resources attributed to the majority of social workers being women who come from the middle class (see Johnson 1972; Toren 1976); and its lack of control over who practices social work (Toren 1972).

The Assessment of Social Worker Autonomy. Although we do not have comparable data from our sixties' sample, social workers' perceptions of their own autonomy and decision-making authority were measured in 1984. The items used in this study were taken from Hall's (1968) research effort to measure various occupational groups' perceptions of their autonomy, and of bureaucratic dimensions in their organizations. The factor analysis that Reeser employed to choose her component items required that she use two items from Hall's autonomy scale, two items from his hierarchy of authority scale, and one item from his rules scale. Using these items we were able to compute an index of autonomy for social workers in the eighties. It is not surprising that the bureaucratic items were highly intercorrelated with the autonomy items in that they addressed the barriers or conditions conducive to achieving autonomy. A score of "high" was given to those who were in the top third of the sample.

Table 3.7 shows the percentage of social workers in 1984 who agreed with each statement about the degree of autonomy they experience in the worksite. Fully 68 percent of the social workers in the eighties scored "high" on autonomy. This compares with Forsyth and Danisiewicz's finding in a national survey of students preparing for eight occupations that social work students scored high on autonomy from the employing organization. In fact, they scored higher than law students (1985:70). On the other hand, the social work practitioners in Hall's study (1968:19) did not perceive themselves to be autonomous in the worksite. The difference in findings may be an indication of increased autonomy for social workers in the eighties.

Answers to individual items in table 3.7 show that only a minority of social workers in the eighties agree there is little autonomy in their work (19%), that they have little opportunity to implement their ideas (20%), that all their decisions have to have the supervisor's approval (16%), or that there are rules for everything in their organization (32%). And while a

TABLE 3.7. Percentage in 1984 Agreeing with Statements About Autonomy in the Work Setting

Degree of Autonomy	*1984*
There is Little Autonomy in My Work	19%
When Problems Arise, There Is Little Opportunity To Implement My Ideas	20
Going Through Proper Channels at all Times Is Stressed	53
There Is a Rule for Everything	32
Any Decision I Make Has To Have the Supervisor's Approval	16
N =	672

little over half (53%) did agree that they have to go through proper channels at work, the profile that emerges from their responses to the complete set of items suggests that social workers in the eighties experience relatively high autonomy in their work.

Clearly, these findings run counter to the earlier theories and majority of studies cited. At least insofar as their perceptions are concerned, social workers in the eighties are highly autonomous. In fact, in response to an individual item that was not included in the autonomy index, 52 percent of the social workers in 1984 agree that, "I know that in my work my own judgement is the final judgement."

Although social workers may be more subject to bureaucratic authority than doctors or lawyers, there are areas of the social worker's job that do allow for substantial autonomy. And it appears that social workers in the eighties have claimed these areas for their own.

For example, the relationship between the worker and the client is usually not observable and, thus, not directly controllable. As a result, social workers have much more discretionary power in dealing with clients then is generally assumed.

In addition, the complex nature of social work practice is often not reducible to rules and regulations. Along these lines, Lipsky (1980:24) has suggested that even public service workers ultimately function as "de facto policy makers" in their work settings.

In this context, it must also be pointed out that much of the theoretical and empirical research literature which describes social workers as having low autonomy is 10 to 20 years old. During that time the culture of social service agencies may have become more professionalized as well as the orientations that social workers bring to these agencies. Although the explanation warrants additional research, the result seems to be a greater perception of autonomy by social workers than was anticipated.

Physicians, Social Workers, and Perceptions of Autonomy. Surprisingly as well, there is some evidence that, for doctors, employment in a bureaucracy as opposed to private practice may be associated with a greater rather than a lesser perception of autonomy. Thus, in her study of physicians, Engel (1970:19) found that those who worked in moderately bureaucratized settings were more likely to perceive themselves as autonomous than those in private practice. She explained that bureaucracies provide professionals with the resources and a "stimulating intellectual climate" that are not available to private practitioners.

In addition, other studies of the medical profession suggest that physicians exercise much less control over their colleagues (Friedson and Buford 1965) and experience much less discretionary authority (Friedson 1984) than was generally assumed.

One explanation offered for the decreasing autonomy of physicians is the increasing governmental regulation of health care and the increasing corporate dominance of medicine. Together they appear to have eroded the doctors' autonomy and self-regulation. Although physicians probably still have considerably more discretion in performing their work than other workers, they are subject to more formal controls than in the past (Freidson 1984).

Comparing social workers to physicians helps to put into perspective the dynamic and historical relationship between professionalization and organizational autonomy. Each is a matter of relative degree and subject to change over time. Clearly, the medical profession does not have total control over its work and social work is not totally lacking in autonomy. Both are myths.

These recent studies of physicians and ours of social workers raise serious question about much of the "established wisdom" or "scientific knowledge" regarding professionals and bureaucracies. They suggest the need for a fundamental theoretical reformulation and more comparative empirical research regarding the relationship between the two. Both are beyond the scope of this book.

In the concluding portion of this chapter, however, we do consider, among other questions, whether social workers in private practice experience greater or lesser autonomy.

THE PROFESSIONALIZATION OF SOCIAL WORK SEGMENTS

So far our discussion has focused on the professional attributes of social work as a single entity at two critical points in its history. Returning to chapter 1, however, we are reminded that different practice groups within social work differed markedly in the sixties and somewhat in the eighties in their commitment to activism.

In this section we address the following questions: (1) Is social work specialization associated with differences in professionalization? (2) If so, did these differences persist from the sixties through the eighties? (3) Was agency auspice associated with differences in professionalization in the eighties? (4) If so, have these differences persisted over time? (Unfortunately, since we have no comparable data from the sixties, this final question cannot be measured directly.)

In chapter 1, we introduced Bucher and Strauss's (1961) "process" model of the professions. Rather than stressing value consensus as does the "community within community" model (Goode 1957), the former approach posits that occupational segments are distinct in their histories, values, and goals as well as in their practice methods. This suggests the possibility that social work "segments" differ as well in their professional attributes.

Specialization and Professionalization

The above discussion suggests that caseworkers, group workers, and community organizers may differ significantly in their patterns and degrees of professionalization.

Without testing this proposition, some social work writers have speculated about such differences. In the fifties, for example, Kahn (1954) claimed that both casework and group work methods were better developed than were those of community organization. So saying, he questioned whether community organizers even required professional training.

Arguing along similar lines, Kadushin (1959:53) asserted that casework was "the most highly professionalized method of social-work practice." He based his conclusion on the extent to which the casework knowledge base, in contrast with those of group work and community organization, was unique and systematic.

In the sixties, Lubove characterized the history of casework as a continued search for a more professional self-image and a systematic knowledge base (Lubove 1965). Since then, the professional literature has minimized the differences between the segments in an effort to demonstrate the common knowledge base that undergirds social work's claim to professionalization (Stewart 1984).

Our various measures of professionalization allow us to assess the degree to which caseworkers, group workers, and community organizers manifest various attributes of professionalization and how these have changed from the sixties to the eighties.

Table 3.8 (pp. 96–97) shows the percentage of social workers trained in casework, group work, or community organization scoring high on each of the measures of professionalization in 1968 and in 1984.[3]

On examining the findings, one is struck first by the fact that the differences between practice segments were statistically significant for each measure of professionalization in 1968, whereas there was one significant difference in 1984. Thus, on these different attributes of professionalization, social workers were more alike in the eighties than they were in the sixties.

This generalization is dramatically illustrated by the differences on the Billingsley role orientation measure in the sixties as contrasted with the eighties. In 1968 we see that social caseworkers were clearly most professionalized on this measure (33%), group workers next (26%), and community organizers last (7%). At that time, the difference between the highest and lowest scores was 26 percent. By 1984, although all had increased in their commitment to a professional reference group, the difference between the highest and lowest segment was only 9 percent.

In addition, patterns of professionalization were found to vary depending on the measures used. Thus in both the sixties and the eighties, caseworkers were most likely to work in organizations with relatively high proportions of master's degree social workers (46% and 42%, respectively), scored highest on the Billingsley role-orientation measure (33% and 57%, respectively), and scored highest on commitment to values of professionalism (36% and 36%, respectively). Community organizers, on the other hand, were consistently highest on professional participation (46% and 44%, respectively).

By contrast, group workers were consistently lowest in the professionalization of the organizations in which they worked (26% and 29%, respectively), lowest in their commitment to values of professionalism (22% and 18%, respectively), have markedly declined in their professional participation since the sixties (−16%) and increased in their commitment to a professional reference group since the sixties (−22%). On the latter measure, caseworkers increased even more, however (+24%), and community organizers most (+43%). Group workers in 1984 were highest on perception of autonomy in the work setting but there were no significant differences between them, caseworkers, and community organizers (48% vs. 35% vs. 44%, respectively).

These disparate findings underscore the importance of greater understanding of the unique histories of different practice segments and more precise conceptualization of the different aspects of professionalization. And while they support the validity of applying the "process model" of professions to the study of social work, they also suggest that social work may be moving closer to the "community model." The latter inference is based on the fact that the differences in professionalization between practice segments have been sharply reduced since the sixties. It is consistent with efforts that are being made to find a common knowledge base and set of values.

Whether this inference is correct and represents a continuing trend must be left to future research efforts.

Auspice and Professionalization

Just as some social work writers have considered differences in professionalization based on practice method, others have addressed the professional attributes of social workers in different practice settings. By contrast to the work on differences by practice method, the work on auspice is based on empirical research.

In the sixties, for example, Cohen (1966:93), claimed that private practitioners were highly professionalized and represented the "elite of the profession" because in his survey of NASW members he found that com-

TABLE 3.8. Percentage in 1968 and 1984 Scoring High on Professionalization by Segment

	Casework 1968	Group Work 1968
Organizational Professionalization	46%[b]	26%[b]
Participation	31[a]	44[a]
Billingsley Professional Role Orientation	33[a]	26[a]
Values of Professionalism[a]	36	22
Autonomy	—	—
N =	731	107

a. $p < .05$.
b. $p < .001$.

pared to other social workers they had more extensive training, experience, and held higher level positions in their work settings.

Similarly, Levenstein (1964:126) concluded from a study of private practitioners that they held more responsible positions than other social workers at both the chapter and national levels of NASW. Most agency social workers, Levenstein went on to say, may belong to NASW but "their participation is limited to payment of dues and occasional attendance at meetings."

In the seventies, Wallace (1977:76) found that one in ten private practitioners either are committee chairs or held office in social work professional associations. He (1982:264) also found private practitioners to be highly professionalized in regard to their pursuit of continuing education well beyond the master's degree.

Despite the absence of comparable data in this study to directly assess differences in professionalization by auspice in the sixties and in the eighties, these studies strongly suggest that private practitioners are likely to score highest on each of our measures of professionalization.

Table 3.9 shows the percentage within each auspice scoring high on each of the measures of professionalization in 1984. In this table, private practitioners are compared with those employed in public, voluntary sectarian, and voluntary nonsectarian agencies.

Not surprisingly, our findings indicate that private practitioners were more likely than other social workers to work in settings in which all other

Community Organization 1968	*Casework 1984*	*Group Work 1984*	*Community Organization 1984*
42%[b]	42%	29%	32%
46[a]	37	28	44
7[a]	57	48	50
29	36	18	22
—	35	48	44
28	425	46	32

TABLE 3.9. Percentage Scoring High on Professionalization by Auspice (1984)

	Private Practice	Public	Voluntary: Sectarian	Voluntary: Nonsectarian
Organizational Professionalization[b]	70%	31%	23%	41%
Participation[a]	51	34	52	30
Bilingsley Professional Role Orientation	55	50	54	64
Autonomy[b]	59	26	39	46
Values of Professionalism	37	33	26	29
$N=$	79	327	44	120

a. $p < .01$.
b. $p < .001$.

social workers have at least an MSW degree (70%). They were virtually the same as those in voluntary sectarian agencies in being most likely to score high on participation in the profession (51% versus 52%, respectively) and, in contrast to Engel's (1970) group of physicians in private practice, they were most likely to score high in the perception of themselves as autonomous in the work setting (59%). (All of these differences by auspice were significant at the .01 level or better.) They were also more likely to be committed to the values of professionalism (37%), but the differences by auspice were not significant.

Only on the measure of professional reference group were private practitioners not highest. On this measure, however, the differences between auspices were not statistically significant.

It is perhaps noteworthy as well that social workers in voluntary sectarian agencies reported the lowest level of organizational professionalization (23%); that those in voluntary nonsectarian agencies were least likely to score high on participation in professional activities (30%); and that social workers in public agencies were least likely to score high on perception of themselves as autonomous in their work (26%). The latter group was also last or next to last on all the other measures of professionalization as well.

Interestingly, although social workers in public agencies are active in lobbying for licensure and against declassification (see chapter 1), they tend to score quite low on attributes of professionalization. Consequently, their efforts may be interpreted as attempts to raise their own or their agency's level of professionalization or, at least, to protect it against further erosion through declassification.

Overall, the previous studies cited and our findings suggest that in the eighties the major differences in professionalization by practice auspice were between private practitioners and those working in traditional agency settings. The former are consistently high on the level of professional education represented in their worksite, professional participation, and perception of autonomy. This pattern appears to have persisted since the sixties.

SUMMARY

In this chapter, we considered the relative extent of social work professionalization in the two eras. In doing so, we applied the "attribute approach," looking at the degree to which social workers' scores have changed on several key indices of professionalization and of professionalism at these two critical junctures in social work history. The dimensions measured were: (1) the level of professional education attained by social workers in the organizational settings in which they were employed; (2) the extent of participation in professional activities and development of knowledge; (3) the degree of commitment to a professional reference group or role-orientation; (4) the degree of commitment to an ideology of professionalism; and (5) the perception of autonomy in one's work situation.

The findings in this chapter suggest that the answer to the question "how professional was social work in the eighties as compared with the sixties?" depends, to a large extent, on how one measures professionalization.

With regard to organizational professionalization, the answer is ambiguous. For while there is a statistically significant decline in the percent of individuals in social work positions possessing master's degrees, it must be remembered that, since the sixties, the entry level degree has shifted to the Bachelor of Social Work. Consequently, if we include BSWs in the percentage of people in social work positions with "professional training," we find it has increased.

Insofar as professional participation is concerned, social workers in the eighties appear to have maintained a relatively high level of conference attendance and to have increased their readership of professional journals. However, their rates of conference presentation and publication efforts seem to have declined. The latter findings may reflect lower psychological involvement in the profession or lesser, per capita, opportunity to present and publish.

The findings with regard to professional reference group and role orientation are clear and unambiguous. Here social workers appear to be increasingly committed to their colleagues as a reference group. Moreover, they remain highly committed to their clients and agencies, and highly resistant to external community influentials who might challenge these commitments.

Whether their bureaucratic commitments are increasing or decreasing depends upon the measures employed. And, while the theoretical relationship between professionalization and bureaucratization seems to be in need of reformulation, social workers of the eighties were clearly more oriented to their professional colleagues than their sixties predecessors were.

Often we confuse the process of professionalization with the ideology of professionalism. The former is a sociological process, the latter a set of social-psychological attitudes, beliefs and values that are linked to the aspiration to professional status.

Our effort to measure social worker's commitment to this ideological dimension suggests that social workers in the eighties were no more committed to an ideology of professionalism than they were in the sixties. If anything, they are less committed to the belief that their problem definitions are superior to those of their low-income clients Consequently, while their commitment to their colleagues as a professional reference group has increased, their endorsement of "professionalist" attitudes has not.

Finally, social workers in the eighties appear to possess a much greater perception of autonomy in their work than was expected. Together with the changing role-orientation patterns, these findings run counter to Epstein and Conrad's (1978:178) description of social workers as mere "organizational functionaries." Instead, social work and social workers appear to be collectively and individually involved in an authentic professionalization process.

This interpretation is supported as well by the analysis of multiple attributes of professionalization by social work specialization. Here, the evidence suggested an increasing professional homogeneity among social workers in the eighties as compared with the sixties.

When multiple attributes of professionalization are considered in relation to practice auspice, the relatively high level of professionalization of private practitioners found in the sixties and seventies, appears to have persisted into the eighties.

In this chapter, as in chapter 1, the importance of historical trends as well as differences among social work practice segments is apparent. What this chapter adds is the recognition that professionalization is a complex and dynamic process that can affect different practice segments differently over the course of history.

Those interested in using the "attribute approach" to further explore the professionalization of social workers (or any other occupational group) are, on the basis of our findings and theoretical speculations, advised to employ a "multi-attribute, historical, process approach" to get the clearest possible picture of this complex process.

In the next chapter, how these different professional attributes effect social worker activism is explored.

4

Professionalization and Social Worker Activism: Two Tests of the "Conservative Professional Community" Model

We remarked at the outset that social workers have long been concerned that increasing professionalization of social work as an institution and of social workers as individuals would decrease and possibly destroy their historic commitment to social activism in behalf of the poor. With regard to this concern, the evidence presented thus far in our study is mixed.

So, while we have presented evidence in the previous chapter of increasing social work professionalization over the past two decades, we have also shown in chapter 1 that social workers in the eighties were more likely to view poverty in social-structural terms and to approve conflict strategies, and were also more politically active through institutionalized channels than their sixties predecessors.

On the other hand, consistent with predictions about the conservatizing effects of professionalization, social workers in the eighties were less likely to engage in protest and to work with or prefer working with the poor.

How these inconsistent political patterns will reconcile themselves as the process of social work professionalization unfolds must be left for future researchers to describe. And, whether the lesser involvement in protest in the eighties or in work with the poor is causally linked to increased professionalization or is merely a reflection of a more conservative historical period is impossible to say at this time.

In this chapter, however, we consider the social action correlates of greater professionalization for individual social workers rather than for social work as a whole. In other words, rather than asking whether social workers as a group have become more or less activist as a result of professionalization, we ask whether those individuals within social work who are more professionalized are also less activist.

More precisely, we ask a series of empirically testable questions related to a theory which has been called the "conservative professional community" model of social work (Epstein 1969). This theoretical model, derived from a rich historic but empirically untested discourse (within social work and sociology) on the negative effects of professionalization, posits that professions constitute communities which are organized around a set of attitudes, beliefs, and values that are conservative in their consequences.

This model assumes that social work constitutes a professional community organized around an elitist ideology of professionalism which emphasizes political and affective neutrality, professional decorum, professional self-regulation, and social distance from the poor. Involvement in this community and commitment to its central ideology, in turn, is assumed to be associated with lesser activism. If these assumptions are correct, individual social workers who are more committed to their professional community will be more committed to an ideology of professionalism and less activist on behalf of the poor. We test these ideas within each of our 1968 and 1984 samples of social workers and compare the findings with each other. Before doing so, however, we must first describe the theoretical underpinnings of these empirical tests.

NEGATIVE THEORIES OF PROFESSIONALIZATION

Ever since individuals began to speculate about the effects of professions in society, sociological and social work theorists alike have warned of the conservative effects of professionalization. While offering different theoretical explanations for their dire predictions, their theories were characterized by what Gouldner (1961:71–82), in the context of organizational theory, has dramatically termed a "negative metaphysical pathos."

Thus, for example, Marxist and neo-Marxist critics of the professions have always regarded professionalization as potentially detrimental to the interests of the proletariat and to the evolution of a progressive society. They have traditionally viewed professions and aspiring professions as supporting the status quo in their attempt to maintain or acquire power and status in the class system.

So even before social workers were worrying about "function" replacing "cause," the sociologist Langerock (1915:44), in a comparative analysis of the professions, argued that the "slum-proletariat" were especially vulnerable to "professional deformation" which he characterized as an exaggerated sense of importance which the professional attached to his or her work, the belief among professionals that they are members of a superior class, and the opposition of such professionals to social change.

Four decades later, C. Wright Mills (1953) predicted that the consequence of professionalization for white-collar workers was political passivity. According to him, white-collar professions offered their members "no steady discontent or responsible struggle with the conditions of their lives." As a result, they became "rearguarders" in progressive political movements rather than risking their newly acquired power and prestige (1953:353–354).

In his study of the medical profession, Freidson (1970:151–155), argued that the values and attitudes inherent in professionalization lead to emphasis on the prestige of the occupation, its position in the class system and in the market, "professional pride," and feelings of superiority. For him, the consequences of professionalization are professional imperialism, narrowness of vision, and lack of concern for the public good.

Looking at how professions organized themselves to obtain market power, Larson (1977) characterized professionalization as a process of creation and control of a market for the services of an occupation, the assertion of high status, and upward social mobility. She argued that professions conform to the social order because of their concern with maintaining status. In so doing, they interpret social problems as private and personal, calling for individual rather than collective solutions. The latter, according to Larson, are regarded as "utopian" by the professions (1977:225).

In a rare empirical study of public health professions, Walsh and Elling (1972) demonstrated that members of those occupational groups who were actively striving to gain higher status for the occupation were more negative in their orientation toward low-income patients than were members of occupations who were less actively striving.

Within social work, but thinking along similar lines, Bisno (1956:17) cautioned social workers against "assuming the rightness and naturalness" of the trend toward greater professionalization. In so doing, he goes on to say, "we have tended to ignore the question of the price to be paid for the higher status and whether it is 'worth' it. Does it imply a weakening of the social in social work?"

Other social work theorists who shared Bisno's concern occupied themselves less with whether or not their negative prediction was correct than with its "explanation." Generally, they offered two types of explanations for the prediction that greater professionalization results in decreased activism: those based on stratification variables (e.g., class, social mobility) and those based on professional attitudes, beliefs, and norms. Although conceptually distinct, these two explanatory hypotheses are often linked by theorists who assume that individual aspiration to upward mobility or what Reeser (1986:128) has called "professional striving" expresses itself in professional attitudes, beliefs, and norms.

Stratification Explanations

Stratification theorists have suggested that the presumed conservative effects of professionalization in social work was a consequence of "collective mobility." These explanations refer to the attitudes held by and the behaviors members of an occupation engage in to move their occupation "up in the hierarchy by turning it into a profession" (Hughes 1958:44–45).

Thus, Benthrup (1964:16) expressed concern about social workers' "selfish interest in acquiring the status symbols of old-line professions" (e.g., private practice) and avoidance of the "basic reasons for the existence of the professions"—serving the poor.

Cloward and Epstein (1965) suggested that a social class conflict exists between middle-class social workers aspiring to professional status and low-income clients. The result, they argued, was social workers' "disengagement from the poor."

Also writing in the sixties, Thursz (1966:13) asserted that "the social work profession cannot allow its preoccupation with status and with the acquisition of various professional attributes or artifacts to hinder its full commitment to social action and social reform."

In the seventies, Wagner and Cohen (1978:50) claimed that the professional striving of social workers resulted in abandoning social reform and energy directed toward "licensure and third party reimbursement, rather than issues that affect the oppression of poor, disadvantaged, and minority peoples."

As the eighties entered, Howe (1980:190) reasoned that the 1979 revision of the social work code of ethics may have signified a return to the "private medical-type model" for social work in its efforts to attain professional status. Her argument was based on the greater number of references in the code to the social worker's primary obligation being to individuals rather than to social change.

Explanations Based on Professional Attitudes, Beliefs, and Norms

Other explanations commonly offered for the presumed linkage between conservatism and professionalization in social work involve the attitudes, beliefs, and norms that are attached to the process of professionalization.

Some, for example, have argued that in its efforts to professionalize social work adopted a knowledge base rooted in Freudian psychology and psychiatry. These theorists suggested that this knowledge base took the social worker's attention away from the sociocultural environment and focused it on the individual psyche. Thus, social reform was repudiated (see Bisno 1956; Woodroofe 1962; Lubove 1965; Berenzweig 1971; Howe 1980).

With the movement away from Freudianism and the adoption of person-in-environment approaches to practice (Germain 1973), such arguments are less commonly heard today.

Nevertheless, there remain many social work critics who view its theory and practice as inherently conservative. Galper (1975:88–91), for example, has argued that social work theory and practice maintains the status quo because the assumptions on which they are based "accept what exists in the society as being on the whole both inevitable and proper."

Linking social work theory and practice to the process of professionalization, neo-Marxist theorists describe social work as supportive of the dominant values in society. Consequently, according to their radical critique, most social workers are simply agents of social control (see Galper 1975; Wagner and Cohen 1978; Heraud 1973; Wilding 1982).

For others, commitment to the intrinsic values, beliefs and norms of professions is regarded as having conservative political implications. Thus, for example, Wilensky and Lebeaux (1965:330) reasoned that social workers who conform to the professional norms of emotional neutrality and functional specificity disclaim their own "humanitarian sentiments" and become preoccupied with technique at the expense of social change. For them, "the forces creating professionalism override individual orientations toward reform (326)."

Similarly, a number of critics of social work professionalization have focused on the preoccupation with "technical professionalism" and the consequent neglect of social problems (see Schorr 1959; Galper 1975; Grønbjerg, Street, and Suttles 1978; Wilding 1982).

Finally, concern has been expressed about the conservative effects of commitment to the norm of professional neutrality. Thus, talking about social work executives, Heffernan (1964) has suggested that adherence to this norm is linked to a desire to protect the professional image of social work and to avoid social action. In quite another context, Piven (1966:78) has remarked that community organizers' deference to the "dictates of professional neutrality" reduces the possibility of politically activating low-income people.

POSITIVE THEORIES OF PROFESSIONALIZATION

Although most of the theorizing about the political effects of professionalization, in social work and in the society at large, has stressed the negative, some sociologists and fewer social workers have described professionalization as a positive and progressive force. These theorists reject the notion that there is an inherent conflict between professionalization and social reform. Indeed, they view professionalization as fostering social change in ways that minimize social conflict and dislocation.

For example, the noted sociologists of the professions, Carr-Saunders and Wilson (1933:284) regarded the professions as possessing special competencies that "are not only not incompatible with the public interest but may be said to promote it."

Durkheim (1933:29, 401) emphasized the integrative function that occupational groups perform for society. He stated that the consequences of professions for society were that they fostered the "general health of the social body" and were the "foundation of the moral order."

Parsons (1964:434) theorized that what set the professions apart from other occupations was their unique integration of the norms of professional achievement with client aid and societal betterment. Through this "collectivity orientation" the interests of the public, the profession, and the client are equated and institutionally reinforced.

Halmos (1970:57) agreed with Durkheim and Parsons about the integrative and moral functions of the professions. He predicted that altruistic "personal service professions" (social work, clinical psychology, etc.) would through professionalization bring about "a major change in the moral climate of society as a whole."

Marshall (1965:159–161) claimed that professionals had a mission "to find for the sick and suffering democracies a peaceful solution of their problems." For him professionalization was a process that produced social change which, at the same time, reduced social class conflict. Similarly, Mannheim (1936:159) viewed the entry of "intellectuals" [read "professionals"] into the political arena as having the positive consequence of transforming "conflict of interests into the conflict of ideas."

Writing in the sixties, Moynihan (1965:13) described the anti-poverty program as a product of the "professionalization of social reform": a program instituted at the behest of professionals rather than the poor, and shaped by professional knowledge rather than by political pressure.

Within social work, Billups (1984:174–175) has asserted that treatment of individual clients and changing of social institutions are characteristic of the "simultaneous dual focus on person-environment interchange" in the professional practice of social work. Similarly, Cooper (1977:361) argued that social work professionals are "change agents" who are "uniquely capable of moving from a case to a cause." Professionalization based on this unique capacity would presumably foster rather than inhibit social change.

Clearly advocates of social work professionalization would be expected to emphasize its positive aspects. Thus, when past presidents of the National Association of Social Workers (NASW) were interviewed regarding the most significant accomplishments of the organization, they all mentioned establishing a professional identity and effective involvement in social action (*NASW News,* October 1985). Paralleling the words of Carr-Saunders and Wilson, these social work leaders view the establishment of a professional identity and commitment to social action as not only not incompatible but actually complementary.

ABSENCE OF EMPIRICAL TESTING

Whether positive or negative, what is striking about this rich tradition of theory and rhetorical dialogue is the almost complete absence of empirical testing of these theories, predictions, and explanations.

Outside of social work, there is the Walsh and Elling (1972) study cited above. Within social work, aside from the work of the present authors, we have found only one empirical study regarding the relationship between professionalization and activism. In that study, Potter (1979) surveyed 140 social workers employed at community mental health centers located throughout the United States. She found no statistically significant relation-ship between social workers' professionalization and their commitment to activism in the community mental health center. Her study is limited, however, by the single field of practice of her subjects, a single measure of professionalization, and the limited context in which social action commit-ment was measured. These limitations may account for Potter's failure to find a relationship between professionalization and activism. Or, there may in fact be no relationship between these two dimensions despite theory and rhetoric to the contrary.

In this chapter, we consider the relationships between several measures of professionalization and several measures of activism. We do this within the context of the theoretical model derived from the social work literature, on two large samples of social workers at two critical junctures in social work history—the sixties and the eighties.

THE "CONSERVATIVE PROFESSIONAL COMMUNITY" MODEL

Earlier in this book, we made reference to one of the most influential articles in the sociology of the professions, that is, Goode's (1957) piece on professions as "communities within the community." Defining community as social rather than physical in its nature, he argued that its members manifest a lasting sense of identification with the profession, a core of common values, agreed upon role definitions, a common language, and control over the selection of trainees and their socialization into the com-munity.

Greenwood (1957) employed Goode's criteria to support the claim that social work was indeed a profession. Writing at a time when social workers were vigorously pursuing professionalization, Greenwood himself and many within social work welcomed this assertion as a very positive statement.

Ironically, the assumption of an integrated professional community is also implicit in the writings of critics of social work professionalization. They argue, however, that the community is organized around a central core of professionalist attitudes, beliefs, and norms which are conservative in their consequences and result in a lesser commitment to activism.

Epstein (1969) translated these implicit assumptions into an empirically testable model of social work as a "conservative professional community." The model contains three basic tenets or theoretical propositions: (1) social work possesses the attributes of an integrated professional community; (2) the professional community is organized around an ideology of professionalism which emphasizes political and affective neutrality, professional self-regulation, and social distance from the poor; (3) to the extent that the first two propositions are correct, social workers who are more committed to their professional community will be less committed to activism in behalf of the poor.

Empirically Testing the "Conservative Professional Community" Model

After translating the model into the three theoretical propositions stated above, Epstein (1969) proposed testing them by looking at the TAU-C intercorrelations among and between various measures of professionalization, professionalism, and social worker activism. The analysis that follows employs the same strategy.

Correlational Analysis

For the reader who is relatively unsophisticated in the use of statistics, it is sufficient to know that Kendall's TAU-C is a measure of association that indicates how two rank-ordered variables (e.g., variables ranked into low, medium, and high categories) are related to each other. Like most other correlation measures, it ranges from -1.00 to 0.00 to $+1.00$. Where a finding falls on this continuum reflects the strength and the direction of a relationship between two variables.

In the context of this study, for example, a correlation of $+1.00$, between organizational professionalization and professional participation would mean that everyone who scored high on organizational professionalization also scored high on professional participation, everyone who scored medium on the former scored medium on the latter, and the remaining individuals were all low on both variables. This unlikely finding would represent a "perfect positive correlation." It is viewed as "perfect" not because it is so desirable, but because it would allow for "perfect" prediction about how one variable was related to the other. Put more simply, knowing that the correlation was $+1.00$ would mean that for virtually every social worker in the sample, we could accurately predict their level of professional participation if we knew the degree of professionalization of their employing organization.

Nor does the term "positive" imply the desirability of this finding. A "positive" or "direct" correlation simply means that the higher an individual scores on one measure, the higher he or she will score on the other.

Alternatively, a correlation of -1.00 between organizational professionalization and professional participation would represent a "perfect negative correlation." Such a finding would mean that every social worker in our sample who worked in a highly professionalized agency, scored low in their professional participation and everyone who worked in an agency characterized by low professionalization was highly active in professional activities.

Such an anomalous finding would still be "perfect" because it would allow for perfect predictability. It would be "negative" or "inverse" because higher scores on one dimension were associated with lower scores on the other.

Perfect or even near-perfect correlations never occur in sociological research, unless we are using correlational measures for testing the reliability of research instruments or for empirically establishing the validity of a theoretical construct such as professionalization. In such instances, one would expect and even require high correlations.

However, in testing hypotheses about attitudes and behaviors such as those related to professionalization and activism, in the real world, where there are so many potential determinants of activism, correlations are likely to be far less than perfect. More likely, they will hover around .00. Such "perfect" noncorrelations would mean that variables are completely unrelated to each other. Consequently, knowing an individual's score on one would add nothing to our ability to predict his or her score on the other.

Statistical significance indicates the degree to which the association found could have occurred by chance alone. The 5 percent level of significance has been defined by convention to be a reasonably rare, chance occurrence. It indicates that less than 5 times out of 100 the relationship occurred by chance. Researchers have generally thought that if significance is .05 or less it is safe to assume that what is found in the study sample can be generalized to the population from which the sample was drawn.

A final reminder is that measures of correlation, in a nonexperimental study of this kind, do not demonstrate which variable caused the other to happen or even which came first. For that, we must rely on theory and logic. This is what researchers mean when they say that "correlation does not mean causation." Instead, together with theory and temporal logic, correlational analysis only suggests causal possibilities.

With this mini-course in correlational analysis completed, we can proceed with testing the "conservative professional community" model. However, for the reader who desires a more technical discussion of Kendall's TAU-C and its uses we recommend Loether and McTavish (1980:227–237) or any basic statistics text.

Is Social Work an Integrated Professional Community?

In the previous chapter, we showed that social workers in the sixties scored relatively low on several measures of professionalization, but that some of these scores significantly increased in the eighties. To determine whether social work constituted a "structurally integrated" professional community during either of those periods we consider the correlations among our various measures of professionalization.

Following Landecker's (1951) seminal paper on "Types of Integration and Their Measurement," March and Simon's (1958:70–71) theoretical discussion on the expected interrelationships among various elements of professionalization, Benguigui's (1967) methodological approach to assessing the professionalization of engineers in France, and Epstein's (1969) earlier work on social worker professionalization, we would argue that to the extent that social work constituted an "integrated professional community" the model would predict high positive correlations among all of our measures of professionalization.

In other words, social workers who worked in highly professionalized organizations would participate actively in professional activities; those who participated highly would score high on professional role-orientation; and so on.[1]

Table 4.1 (opposite page) shows the TAU-C correlations among each pair of our measures of professionalization for the 1968 sample and table 4.2 (p. 116) shows the correlations for the 1984 sample. Reeser's (1986) measure of professional autonomy is included for the 1984 sample. This was not employed in the 1968 survey.

For social workers in the 1968 sample, of the three paired relationships among the structural attributes of professionalization suggested by the community model, none are significantly correlated. Thus, despite our theoretical prediction of relatively high correlations, the actual findings were all very close to .00. We can only conclude on the basis of the evidence presented that social work was not a structurally integrated professional community in the sixties.

For social workers in the 1984 sample, of the six paired relationships

TABLE 4.1. Tau-C Intercorrelations of Indices of Professionalization for 1968[a]

	Organizational Professionalization	Partici- pation	Billingsley Professional Role Orientation	Values of Profession- alism
Organizational Profession- alization	—	.02	.05	−.02
Participation	—	—	−.06	.05
Billingsley Professional Role Orientation	—	—	—	−.07

a. *N*s range from 826 to 899 when no answers (NAs) are excluded from the analysis.

among structural attributes of professionalization, five are statistically significant and positive in direction. The strength of these correlations is quite weak however. More specifically, organizational professionalization is positively associated with professional participation (+ .08), commitment to a professional role orientation (+ .12) and perception of autonomy (+ .10). Perception of autonomy is also positively correlated with professional participation (+ .10) and professional role orientation (+ .07). Only the Billingsley Role-Orientation measure was unrelated to Professional Participation (+ .02).

Although the strength of the correlations in the 1984 sample are quite weak, when combined with our findings of increased professionalization in the eighties, described in the previous chapter, their consistency and direction suggest that social work in the eighties has not only acquired more of the attributes of a profession as compared with the sixties but also that these attributes are more structurally integrated in the eighties. In addition indirect support for this conclusion is lent by our earlier findings of decreased differentiation of the professional attributes of caseworkers, group workers, and community organizers in the eighties.

In other words, despite claims of complete professionalization (Greenwood 1957) and counter-claims of deprofessionalization (Epstein and Conrad 1978), social work appears closer to having achieved a state of "professional community" in the eighties than it had in the sixties. Nevertheless, using our empirical assessment criteria of professionalization, the weakness of the correlations suggests that there is still a long way to go until the process is fully integrated into the professional attitudes, behaviors and agency environments of most social workers.

However positive for advocates of professionalization, these findings negate the first tenet of the "conservative professional community" model for social workers in the sixties, but partially support it in the eighties. Thus, in answer to our first question, social work appears to have been more of a structurally integrated professional community in the eighties than it was in the sixties. However, this process of structural integration is by no means completed or even strongly advanced.

Is the Professional Community of Social Workers Organized Around an Ideology of Professionalism?

The second tenet of the "conservative professional community" model is that the professional community of social workers is organized around a professionalist ideology that stresses political and affective neutrality, decorum, professional self-regulation, and social distance from the poor.[2] Put in empirically testable terms, this model would predict strong positive correlations between the structural attributes of professionalization and commitment to the ideology of professionalism. More specifically social workers who work in more professionalized organizations, participate more in professional activities, have more professional role orientations, and experience greater professional autonomy will be more committed to an ideology which stresses neutrality, decorum, and social distance from low-income clients.

These ideas are tested in table 4.1 for social workers in the sixties and in table 4.2 for social workers in the eighties. Contrary to the predictions based on the "conservative professional community" model, the empirical evidence in both samples indicates no positive association between the structural attributes of professionalization and commitment to a professionalist ideology. In fact, in the 1984 sample, those who experience high levels of professional autonomy are slightly but significantly lower in their commitment to this ideology $(-.07)$.

These findings lead us to reject the second tenet of the "conservative professional community" model. They are consistent with Hall's (1968) research in comparative study of the professions. He found that the structural (e.g., professional association, code of ethics) and attitudinal aspects (e.g., belief in self-regulation, service ideal) of professionalization were not necessarily correlated.

The findings also lend empirical support to Vollmer and Mills' (1966) theoretical contention that ideologies of professionalism are not by definition linked to achievement of the structural elements of professionalization. In other words, there is little or no relationship between the extent that individuals or occupations are professionalized and the extent to which they espouse a professionalist ideology.

Are Social Workers Who Are More Professionalized Also Less Activist?

The final tenet of the "conservative professional community" model is that social workers who are more highly professionalized will be less activist than their less professionalized peers. In other words, those who are most involved in professional community by virtue of their organizational environments, extra-organizational activities, and reference group orientations, will be most likely to reject activism in behalf of the poor.

Put in testable terms, those who work in more professionalized organizations, participate more in professional activities, have higher professional role orientations, and experience greater professional autonomy will be less likely to endorse activist goals, support activist strategies, and engage in activist behaviors. In contrast with the previous sets of correlational hypotheses, here the "conservative professional community" model would predict strong negative correlations between our structural measures of professionalization and our attitudinal and behavioral measures of activism.

As we indicated earlier however, the theoretical explanation offered for this prediction is that the neutralist ideology "inherent" in professionalization will predispose more professionalized social workers to reject activism. However, we have already shown that the ideology of professionalism is not only not inherent in professionalization but is actually unrelated to it. Irrespective of its possible explanation, the next question to be answered (and possibly the central question of this study) is whether professionalization itself is inversely related to activism as the "conservative professional community" model would suggest.

Table 4.3 (p. 118) presents the TAU-C correlations between our measures of professionalization and our measures of activism for social workers in 1968. Table 4.4 (p. 118) does the same for the 1984 sample. Of 12 possible tests of the predicted inverse relationship between professionalization and social worker activism in 1968, none was significantly correlated in the direction predicted by the model. Of 24 tests of the relationship between professionalization and social activism in 1984, only one was significantly related in the predicted direction. Thus, for social workers in the eighties there was a weak but statistically significant negative relationship between organizational professionalization and participation in institutionalized social action behavior (TAU-C = $-.11$).

In both samples, the preponderance of evidence suggests that for individual social workers greater professionalization is not associated with lesser activism as the "conservative professional community" model predicts. In fact, in 1968 and 1984, several statistically significant findings run counter to the prediction.

Thus, we see that in 1968 those social workers who were more likely to participate in professional association activities were also more likely to participate in institutionalized forms of social action behavior (TAU-C = $+.32$). In addition, in 1968 organizational professionalization was significantly associated with greater support for conflict strategies in public welfare (TAU-C = $+.12$).

In 1984, professional participation was significantly correlated with institutionalized social action behavior (TAU-C = $+.25$), electoral activism (TAU-C = $+.17$), and professional lobbying and licensing activities (TAU-C = $+.24$). Finally, we see that in 1984 the perception of greater professional

TABLE 4.2. Tau-C Intercorrelations of Indices of Professionalization for 1984[a]

	Organizational Professionalization	*Participation*
Organizational Professionalization	—	.08[c]
Participation	—	—
Billingsley Professional Role Orientation	—	—
Values of Professionalism	.01	−.02

autonomy is weakly but significantly associated with greater participation in protest and electoral activism (TAU-C = +.05 and +.09, respectively).

Although several of these unpredicted positive correlations between professionalization and social worker activism were weak, the strongest and most consistent finding which does emerge in 1968 and 1984 is that greater participation in the professional community through activities such as conference attendance, journal readership, and publication is associated with greater participation in institutionalized forms of social action behavior (e.g., visiting public officials, contributing money to a political campaign, working for social work licensing).

One possible explanation for these findings is that participation in professional activities places individuals in formal networks that provide motivation and opportunity for institutionalized political involvement. In addition, such participation could provide access to informal networks that contribute to solidarity among social workers and offer support for engaging in socially accepted forms of activism. Today NASW strongly encourages its members to participate in the political system and to be involved in licensing and efforts to protect the social work title. Those active in social work organizations may be more likely to carry out these activities.

These findings stop short of demonstrating a positive relationship between participation in the professional community and involvement in non-institutionalized forms of social activism as NASW leaders have suggested.

Billingsley Professional Role Orientation	Values of Professionalism	Autonomy
.12[d]	.01	.10[c]
.02	−.02	.10[c]
—	.03	.07[b]
.03	—	−.07[b]

a. *N*s range from 615 to 682 when NAs are executed from the analysis.
b. $p \leq .05$.
c. $p \leq .01$.
d. $p \leq .001$.

TABLE 4.3. Tau-C Correlations of Social-Work Activism Indices by Professionalization and Values of Professionalism for 1968

	Organizational Professionalization	Partici- pation	Billingsley Professional Role Orientation	Values
Activist Goals	−.01	.05	−.02	−.19[c]
Public Welfare Conflict Approval	.12[b]	−.04	.04	−.19[c]
Institutionalized Social Action Behavior	−.01	.32[c]	.03	−.01
Noninstitutionalized Social Action Behavior	−.01	.02	−.01	−.19[c]

a. Ns range from 826 to 899 when NAs are excluded from the analysis.
b. $p < .01$.
c. $p < .001$.

TABLE 4.4. Tau-C Correlations of Social Work Activism Indices by Professionalization and Values of Professionalism for 1984

	Organizational Professionalism	Participation
Activist Goals	−.02	.05
Public Welfare Conflict Approval	.02	.04
Institutionalized Social Action Behavior	−.11[d]	.25[d]
Noninstitutionalized Social Action Behavior	−.01	.02
Electoral Social Action Behavior	.08[c]	.17[d]
Professional Social Action Behavior	.02	.24[d]

a. Ns range from 607 to 682 when NAs are excluded from the analysis.
b. $p < .05$.
c. $p < .01$.
d. $p < .001$.

For such support, Wagner (1988) has shown that more radical social workers must seek out organizational alternatives to NASW.

Overall, however, in answer to the third question posed by the "conservative professional community" model, we find that more professionalized social workers in the sixties and in the eighties are no less activist than their less professionalized peers. And, in many cases, within institutionalized channels, they are more activist.

HOW DOES COMMITMENT TO AN IDEOLOGY OF PROFESSIONALISM AFFECT SOCIAL WORKERS' ACTIVISM?

Earlier in this chapter we demonstrated that contrary to the claims of the "conservative professional community" model, the structural attributes of professionalization were unrelated to whether social workers endorsed a professionalist ideology. In the previous discussion, we showed that structural measures of professionalization were not associated with lesser activ-

Billingsley Professional Role Orientation	Autonomy	Values
.00	−.04	−.21[d]
.04	−.02	−.16[d]
.03	.04	−.03
.00	.05[b]	−.06[b]
.02	.09[c]	−.17[c]
−.00	.02	−.02

ism. This naturally raises the question, however, of whether commitment to an ideology of professionalism is associated with lesser activism.

Table 4.3 (above) presents the TAU-C correlations between commitment to a neutralist ideology of professionalism and our measures of social worker activism in 1968. Table 4.4 (above) does the same for 1984. In 1968 we see that there is a statistically significant negative relationship between commitment to professionalism on the one hand and endorsement of activist goals (TAU-C = −.19), approval of conflict strategies in public welfare (TAU-C = −.19), and noninstitutionalized social action behavior (TAU-C = −.19).

Table 4.5 translates these correlations into percentages. So, for example, of those social workers in 1968 who scored in the top third on commitment to a professionalist ideology, only 29 percent supported social work organized protest to bring about change in the public welfare system. Of those in 1968 who scored in the bottom third on professionalism, 50 percent endorsed this conflict strategy. Moreover, in 1968 only 17 percent of those with a high commitment to professionalism participated in some form of protest during the past year, as compared to 40 percent of those who were least committed to professionalism.

In table 4.4, we had found similar negative correlations in 1984 between professionalism and commitment to activist goals (TAU-C = −.21), approval of conflict strategies in public welfare (TAU-C = −.16), noninstitutionalized activism (TAU-C = −.06), and electoral activism (TAU-C = −.17).

In table 4.5 the percentage of those social workers in 1984 who scored high on commitment to a professionalist ideology (27%) endorsed activist goals for social work. However, of those scoring low on professionalism, 52 percent endorsed activist goals. Although 22 percent of those most committed to professionalism participated in electoral activism, 45 percent of those least committed to professionalism were actively engaged in electoral activities.

In comparing the sixties and the eighties it is interesting to note, however, that the negative relationship between commitment to professionalism and protest behavior drops from −.19 to −.06. This suggests the possibility that other factors such as diminished opportunities to engage in protest movements may be affecting the noninstitutionalized social action behaviors of social workers in the eighties.

Overall, however, these findings reflect a remarkably consistent pattern, in the sixties and in the eighties, of greater conservatism associated with

TABLE 4.5. Percent in 1968 and 1984 Scoring High on Social Work Activism by Degree of Professionalism[a]

	Values—1968			Values—1984		
	Low	Medium	High	Low	Medium	High
Activist Goals	33%	28%	17%	52%	36%	27%
Public Welfare Conflict Approval	50	41	29	55	51	37
Institutionalized Social Action Behavior	47	50	46	41	38	34
Noninstitutionalized Social Action Behavior	40	31	17	18	20	11
Electoral Social Action Behavior	—	—	—	45	38	22
Professional Social Action Behavior	—	—	—	45	46	42

a. N is 899 for 1968 and Ns range from 653 to 670 when NAs are excluded from the analysis.

endorsement of a professionalist ideology that stresses political and affective neutrality, decorum, professional self-regulation, and social distance from low-income clients. Yet, as we have pointed out, this ideology seems to have little to do with professionalization, per se. Nor does it appear to be central to the professional values of the social work community.

Very likely, rejection of social activism in behalf of the poor because it is "unprofessional" represents a more socially acceptable justification within social work than the direct expression of more conservative political sentiments. The latter are likely to have their origins outside of social work.

TESTING THE "CONSERVATIVE PROFESSIONAL COMMUNITY" MODEL WITHIN SOCIAL WORK SEGMENTS

Although the "conservative professional community" model did not withstand empirical testing with our two samples taken as total groups, it might be argued that if the samples were divided into social work segments the model would be more predictive. In particular, since social casework has long dominated social work as an institution (Lubove 1965), the "conservative professional community" model may effectively describe caseworkers' attitudes and behaviors yet be incorrectly interpreted as reflecting the attitudes and behaviors of all social workers. And, by treating caseworkers and noncaseworkers as a single group, these patterns, it might be argued, are obscured.

To empirically test this idea, we applied the professional community model to caseworkers and noncaseworkers taken as separate groups.[3] This approach assumed that casework might constitute a "conservative professional community" unto itself.

Table 4.6 shows the TAU-C correlations between our measures of professionalization and our measures of activism within segments in 1968 and table 4.7 (pp. 124–25) does the same for the 1984 sample.

Analysis by social work segment of the 1968 data showed no evidence to support the "conservative professional community" model among caseworkers. In fact, caseworkers as well as group workers and community organizers who participate in professional activities were more likely to be involved in institutionalized social action behavior (TAU-C is .26 for case-

TABLE 4.6. Tau-C Correlations Between Social Work Activism and Professionalization Within Segments for 1968

| | Organizational Professionalization | |
	CW	GW & CO
Activist Goals	.02	.26[b]
Public Welfare Conflict Approval	.16[c]	.31[c]
Institutionalized Social Action Behavior	.00	.00
Noninstitutionalized Social Action Behavior	.01	.07
$N =$	654	127

a. The abbreviations CW, GW, and CO are used for casework, group work, and community organization.
b. $p < .05$.
c. $p < .01$.
d. $p < .001$.

workers and .31 for group workers and community organizers). For all segments, only commitment to the values of professionalism was associated with lesser activism.

Interestingly, among group workers and community organizers statistically significant positive correlations were found between organizational professionalization and activist goals (TAU-C = +.26), public welfare conflict approval (TAU-C = +.31), professional participation and institutionalized social action behavior (TAU-C = +.31) and a statistically significant negative correlation (TAU-C = -.24) between organizational professionalization and commitment to a professionalist ideology (see Epstein 1969:88).

This raises the possibility that the norms of highly professionalized antipoverty agencies such as Mobilization for Youth (Brager and Purcell 1967; Weissman 1969) that employed group workers and community organizers in the sixties actually supported activism and protest and actively rejected professionalism.

Analysis of the 1984 data by segments offered no evidence to support the "conservative professional community" model among caseworkers, nor among group workers and community organizers. However, the organiza-

Participation		Billingsley Professional Role Orientation		Values	
CW	*GW & CO*	*CW*	*GW & CW*	*CW*	*GW & CW*
.00	.01	−.01	.06	−.16[d]	−.23[?]
−.05	−.14	.04	.17	−.17[d]	−.1E
.26[d]	.31[c]	.07	−.08	.00	(4
−.05	.08	.00	.10	−.16[d]	−.)€
731	135	731	135	731	13E

tional supports for protest and anti-professionalism among group workers and community organizers that were reflected in the sixties sample was not apparent in the eighties data. This may be a consequence of more conservative times. Or, it may be a conservative consequence of the decreasing differentiation among social work segments found in the eighties. This is a question for future researchers.

Turning to institutionalized types of social action behavior in the eighties by practice segments provides additional evidence of the greater involvement in this type of activism among social workers who participate more in professional activities. Thus, for caseworkers and noncaseworkers alike, there is a statistically significant positive association between professional participation and participation in institutionalized social action behavior (TAU-C is $+.19$ for caseworkers, and $+.16$ for group workers and community organizers), electoral activism (TAU-C is $+.16$ for caseworkers and $+.12$

TABLE 4.7. Tau-C Correlations Between Social Work Activism and Professionalization Within Segments for 1984

	Organizational Professionalization		Participation	
	CW	GW & CO	CW	GW & CO
Activist Goals	.00	.04	.04	.09
Public Welfare Conflict Approval	.05	.06	.01	−.06
Institutionalized Social Action Behavior	−.04	.11	.19[d]	.16[b]
Noninstitutionalized Social Action Behavior	.02	−.02	.04	.00
Electoral Social Action Behavior	.14[d]	.00	.16[d]	.12
Professional Social Action Behavior	.00	.10	.16[d]	.40[d]
N=	386	73	425	78

a. The abbreviations CW, GW, and CO are used for casework, group work, and community organization.
  b. $p < .05$.
  c. $p < .01$.
  d. $p < .001$.

for group workers and community organizers), and professional activism (TAU-C is $+.16$ for caseworkers and $+.40$ for group workers and community organizers). For all segments, only commitment to an ideology of professionalism was associated with lesser activism.

Interestingly, among group workers and community organizers, statistically significant positive correlations were found between professional role orientation and activist goals (TAU-C $= +.22$), public welfare conflict approval (TAU-C $= +.16$), institutionalized social action behavior (TAU-C $= +.22$), and noninstitutionalized social action behavior (TAU-C $= +.17$). No relationships were found for caseworkers. The differences between caseworkers and noncaseworkers suggest that group workers and community organizers find more support from colleagues for endorsing and engaging in more militant activism (e.g., actively organizing welfare recipients to conduct protest demonstrations) and participating in institutionalized activ-

Billingsley Professional Role Orientation		Autonomy		Values	
CW	*GW & CW*	*CW*	*GW & CW*	*CW*	*GW & CO*
.00	.22[b]	−.04	.06	−.18[c]	−.14
.06	.16[b]	−.03	.13	−.11	−.11
.04	.22[c]	.03	.03	−.01	−.10
.03	.17[b]	.08[b]	.02	−.09	−.01
.06	.09	.06	.12	−.25[d]	−.34[b]
.00	−.02	.00	.27[b]	−.07	−.20
414	76	419	76	414	73

ism. Identification with their colleagues as a reference group may contribute to feelings of solidarity and provide reinforcement for risk-taking behaviors and liberal attitudes.

SUMMARY AND CONCLUSIONS

In this chapter we tested the "conservative professional community" model in 1968 and 1984 to see if it accurately describes social workers' professional attitudes, beliefs, and behavior and predicts their activism. This widely held model assumes that social work constitutes a professional community which is organized around an ideological core that emphasizes neutrality, decorum, professional self-regulation, and social distance from the poor. The consequence of involvement in this professional community and commitment to this ideological core is assumed to be greater conservatism and lesser activism among social workers.

Our evidence indicates that this paradigm describes neither the professional structure of social work nor its ideological core and does not adequately predict differences in social worker activism. More specifically, the empirical findings based on the 1968 sample neither support the claim to professional community, nor do they suggest that the attributes of professionalization that do exist are associated with a neutralist professional ideology. Finally, the findings for the sixties negate the popular assertion that greater social worker professionalization is associated with lesser activism.

Analysis of the 1984 data provided some evidence that social work has achieved a minimal state of professional community. In accord with the descriptive comparisons presented in chapter 3, comparisons of the correlational analyses of sixties and eighties data in this chapter suggest a movement in the direction of greater structural integration of this community in the eighties. This movement is far from complete however.

Contrary to the predictions of the "conservative professional community" model, however, more professionalized social workers in 1984 were not more committed to a neutralist ideology of professionalism. Nor were they less activist.

In the sixties, for group workers and community organizers, organizational professionalization was associated with greater support of protest and rejection of professionalism as an ideology. By the eighties this organizational support had disappeared.

However, in the eighties, for group workers and community organizers, identification with colleagues as a primary reference group was associated with greater support of and participation in protest and institutionalized activism. In both time periods, for all segments, commitment to a neutralist ideology was associated with lesser activism, but participation in professional activities was associated with greater institutionalized activism.

The findings in this chapter and in chapter 2 on background characteristics strongly suggest that differences in activism among social workers are likely to be a product of factors independent of professionalization—differential recruitment patterns, different background characteristics, different political affiliations, etc. (Shaw 1985). Because political activism is frequently characterized by more conservative social workers as "unprofessional," however, it is easy to understand why professionalization is commonly viewed as undermining social worker activism.

To be consistent with our findings, we must reject both the positive claims that social work has fully achieved professional community and the negative claims that involvement in this community is conservative in its consequences. Thus, in neither the sixties nor the eighties was data on professionalization associated with lesser commitment to the problems of the poor or lesser involvement in social action.

In the next chapter, we speculate about the future of professionalization and activism and the persistence of the "myth" of their incompatibility.

5

The Mythology and the Future of Social Work Professionalization and Activism

Throughout this book we have referred to social workers' historic ambivalence regarding professionalization and activism. Put simply, their fear has been that pursuing the former meant abandoning the latter. In other words, rejection of programs for the poor and of social action in their behalf is generally thought to be the price of greater professionalization.

In many ways, our purpose here has been to determine whether there is empirical justification for this concern. Our findings suggest that there is little empirical support for the proposition that professionalization, per se, is a conservatizing force in social work. Nor, for that matter, is there support for the claim that social work is, even now, highly professionalized.

On the one hand, these findings depart significantly from the conventional wisdom of professionalization's radical opponents. On the other hand, they fly in the face of social work professionalization's staunchest advocates.

In this chapter, we suggest that the conventional wisdom regarding social work professionalization and its conservatizing consequences is symbolically significant even if it is not statistically significant. Here we are suggesting that such beliefs have institutional importance irrespective of whether or not they are factually correct.

Hence, despite empirical evidence to the contrary, the common assumption that social workers in the sixties were radical activists and that the achievement of professionalization has made social work and social workers more conservative are central elements in the "political mythology" of social work.

This explains why these "cherished" beliefs have persisted historically despite the historical evidence to the contrary. In addition, it explains why they have never before been put to a serious, scientific test. And, very likely, it will explain why these beliefs are likely to be sustained and perpetuated long after this book has been published and read.

This is not meant to imply however, that this book and its findings should put the issues of the future of social work professionalization and social worker activism to rest. In fact, after elaborating on the concept of political mythology and its sociological functions, we raise at least two very real significant dilemmas facing social work in the years to come.

The first has to do with the conflict between different models of professionalization and de-professionalization (or as neo-Marxists view it "proletarianization"). Implicated in this discussion, is the issue of unionization as well.

The second has to do with the future of social worker activism. The issue here is not the conflict between activism and apathy but rather how will social worker activism be expressed in future years.

With regard to both sets of issues, a distinction needs to be made between *predictive* statements concerning how these issues might be resolved versus *prescriptive* statements concerning what the authors think should take place. On the former, the authors generally agree. On the latter, they disagree. To minimize the ideological rhetoric, we limit our discussion to our areas of agreement.

Finally, we conclude with suggestions for future empirical research on these important issues.

THE POLITICAL MYTHOLOGY OF PROFESSIONALIZATION AND ACTIVISM

In his book entitled *The Political Mythology of Apartheid,* Thompson suggests that all political systems generate mythologies that legitimize their existence and survival. In his review of Thompson's book, Bishop Tutu (1985) describes these mythologies as not only ubiquitous but also extremely 'malleable', demonstrating a "remarkable capacity to be adjusted as the circumstances to which they seek to be relevant change" (p.3).

Tutu goes on to describe Thompson's criteria for evaluating a political myth. He comments:

First, how well does it stand up to the critical scrutiny of the historian who uses a rigorous historical method for evaluating the evidence and how consistent is the conclusion with the historical data? Second, how closely does the particular myth agree with scientific knowledge? Can it stand up to close questioning from competent practitioners of the science most relevant to the discussion? And finally what he calls a utilitarian criterion, which does not ask whether the myth is true or not but whether its effects are good or bad (p.3).

Similarly, in his work on the mythology of North American Indians, Bierhorst suggests that the "truth" of sacred beliefs among these indigenous peoples "may be ranked above or even opposed to fact" (Le Guin 1985: 7).

Following Thompson's and Bierhorst's line of reasoning, we would argue that every social institution has its own political mythology, the function of which is to ensure the survival and expansion of that institution despite changing historical circumstances even in the face of conflicting empirical evidence.

For social work, the commonly held beliefs that social workers in the past were more activist, that professional status has been achieved, and finally that professionalization is a conservatizing force are all elements of a liberal political mythology. This mythology maintains a pluralist equilibrium between various potentially conflicting constituencies within social work. In so doing, it allows for the simultaneous support of strategies of social change and professionalization efforts. And, ironically, by emphasizing the conservatizing influence of professionalization it symbolically maintains a commitment to liberal values while asserting the impact and extent of social work professionalization.

Thus far in this book, we have employed the first two of Thompson's criteria for evaluating political mythology; that is, we have focused our attention on the historical and empirical evidence. As a result, we have shown that contrary to social work folklore, social workers in the sixties were not necessarily more activist than those in the eighties and that both sets of social workers were primarily committed to consensus strategies of change. In fact, on some criteria social workers in the eighties were more activist than their predecessors.

Indeed, in a pair of recent special issues of *The Urban and Social Change Review* (Summer and Winter 1985) entitled "Has Social Work Abandoned

Social Welfare?" Austin (1985:16) disputes the "historic truisms" that in the past social workers were linked together by a social commitment and were "overwhelmingly involved in social change efforts." Instead, he argues that "organized social welfare, and the institutional aspects of professional social work, developed primarily as part of a middle-of-the-road progressive reform tradition in the United States that took the free-market, capitalist economic system as a given. Much of the motivation for such efforts was to push social reform as an alternative to socialist political initiatives."

He goes on to make the point that before and during the sixties much of the leadership in protest and reform efforts did not come from social workers. He disputes the claim that social work activism declined in the eighties compared with the sixties.

Moreover he asserts that the major differences in the activism of social workers in the two decades involve different substantive issues rather than fundamentally different political commitments. So, for example, although social workers in the sixties couched their commitments more exclusively in the context of poverty, in the eighties the social action issues were those that transcended social class, such as work with the elderly and the disabled, AIDS, and the like. He implies that social workers' liberal values were much the same in both periods, they were simply channeled differently. Our study suggests that the shape these political impulses took were determined more by historical political trends in regard to protest and more by increased professionalization in regard to institutionalized forms of social action.

The evidence from our study supports Austin's argument. Although social workers in the sixties were more likely to endorse the activist goal of social change in behalf of the poor and were more supportive of protest than their eighties counterparts, the majority were not involved in social activism, were primarily committed to consensus strategies, and were not invested in serving the poor.

Nevertheless, two issues of *The Urban and Social Change Review* were entirely devoted to this question, which underscores its continuing salience and the symbolic significance of this theme within social work.

This turns us to Thompson's "utilitarian" criterion, and naturally raises the question of why social work scholars and nonscholars alike have persistently pointed to professionalization as the major explanation for differences in commitment to activism. Alternatively, we may ask why the influence of specialization and of social worker background characteristics have been generally ignored.

One reason for the emphasis on professionalization is suggested by our earlier finding that in both the sixties and the eighties commitment to an ideology of professionalism is associated with greater conservatism. Although this ideology, which stresses neutrality and social distance from the client, does not appear to be linked to structural measures of social work professionalization, more conservative social workers frequently justify their political positions in terms of this ideology. In other words, they often reject social causes and social action efforts as "nonprofessional" or as potentially damaging to social work professionalization.

While their political positions are likely to be rooted in background characteristics and political beliefs they bring to the field, it would be quite natural for observers of these conservative social workers to "explain" their conservatism in terms of professionalization.

Alternatively, the exclusion of specialization and of such nonprofessional factors as background characteristics can be accounted for in terms of social work's continuing quest for professional status. We have seen, however, that there is not a great deal of empirical evidence to support this claim. Consequently, this assertion, made so vehemently by Greenwood (1957) in the fifties and so often cited as though it had been validated empirically, is another element in the political mythology of social work.

To the extent that differences in specialization and nonprofessional factors are acknowledged as significant determinants of social worker attitudes and behaviors, social work's institutional claim to professional status is undermined.

Perhaps equally important is the recognition that explanations tied to differences in specialization and in background characteristics are potentially disruptive to the internal cohesion of social work as an institution. These explanations are, therefore, not institutionally accepted, since recognition might lead to rancorous conflict within social work. Such acknowledgment might influence recruitment and admission policies and practices in ways that are inconsistent with the law as well as with the ethical values and standards of social work (Shaw 1985). In addition, it could pit caseworkers against community organizers, male social workers against female, Whites against Blacks, Catholics against Jews, and so on.

One fragment of historical evidence that supports this interpretation is contained within Lindeman's Introduction to Bisno's book, *The Philosophy of Social Work* (1952:v-vi). In that book, Bisno describes the conservatism of "Roman Catholic social work." In his Introduction to the book, Lindeman attempts to smooth the ruffled feathers of Catholic social workers who might be offended by Bisno's analysis, by suggesting that Bisno was merely "attempting to clarify his position by comparing his principles with those advocated by Roman Catholic social workers." He goes on to suggest that Bisno might have just as easily used "Lutheran, or Islamic, or Jewish social work" in elaborating his thesis. Finally, Lindeman lauds Bisno for his "courageous enterprise" and urges "those who will be incited to disagreement" to "remain calm."

It becomes clear then that the "common wisdom" and institutionalized beliefs and explanations concerning professionalization and social work activism are linked to the political and professional survival of social work as a collectivity. Irrespective of their historical or empirical truth, they are part of the folklore of social work. As such, they contribute significantly to the maintenance of the institution.

THE FUTURE OF SOCIAL WORK PROFESSIONALIZATION

The foregoing discussion is not to suggest that this study has "closed the book" on the issue of social work professionalization. To the contrary, this study neither predicts the extent to which social work professionalization will develop nor does it suggest the form this professionalization should take.

On the latter point, Leighninger (1986) recently described two very different future models of professionalization proposed by two influential past leaders in social work. Edith Abbott desired that social work emulate the traditional professions of medicine and law. Her image of professionalization emphasized a scientific basis for practice. Within this model the professional organization would serve as gatekeeper imposing restrictive standards for entry into the occupation and would work on improving the quality of training and the image of social work.

As far as social action was concerned, she argued for an expert, nonpartisan role for social workers in the development of social policy. A political moderate, Abbott believed that advocacy should be limited to experts giving testimony and lobbying for social reform within the system.

Like Abbott, Bertha Reynolds stressed a scientific base for social work practice. She differed, however, from Abbott in her perspectives on membership in social work and the role and content of standards. She argued for including the untrained and unskilled in the professional association and for improving their working conditions as well as protecting the rights of clients. Reynolds believed that labor unions could perform this role and professional organizations could perform an educational function. A Socialist and an activist, Reynolds argued that it is the obligation of social workers to take partisan political stands and work for structural changes in the socioeconomic system.

Abbott and Reynolds offered and endorsed fundamentally different models of professionalization. Nevertheless, they each supported the professionalization process.

By contrast, Epstein and Conrad (1978:177) suggested that the heuristic model of social work be de-professionalized. On the basis of their research findings and his neo-Marxist political analysis of social work as an institution, Burghardt (1982:222) proposes the rejection of the professionalization project. He argues that the latter is merely a managerial "ploy" to deflect social workers from the "harsh organizational realities," increased "trivialization," and decreased autonomy experienced by social workers.

More recently, Dressel, Waters, and Sweat (1988: 118–119) cite examples of such "proletarianization" of welfare work as the division of labor into smaller, simpler components that can be accomplished by less skilled, lower paid employees; the switching of emphasis from less tangible casework functions to more measurable forms of service (e.g., meal provision, transportation, etc.); and the increasing supervision and hierarchy all designed to make workers more bureaucratically accountable and less autonomous.

Although proponents of the proletarianization thesis do not endorse this process, they suggest that social workers should recognize the reality of this phenomenon, should reject the "false consciousness" (Mills 1953) that is associated with professionalization movements and, instead, should turn to trade unionism along with other white collar workers (Galper 1975; Larson 1977; Burghardt 1982).

Taking a different position, Alexander (1980) argued that professionalization and unionization are not incompatible. Instead, she suggests that they are incompatible only if they are viewed as alternative "ideal types." She proposes a hybrid model of professional union which draws upon but is different from trade unions and professional associations. In support of her thesis, recent surveys suggest that social workers do not believe that unionization is incompatible with professionalization (Shaffer 1979; Lightman 1982).

Nevertheless, data from the present study indicate that 33 percent of the social workers in the 1968 sample indicated that social workers had a union in their workplace as compared with 24 percent in 1984. (The difference is statistically significant at the .001 level.) Previously cited findings also suggest that social workers in the eighties were more professionalized than their sixties counterparts and perceived themselves as relatively autonomous in their organizational settings (see chapter 3).

These empirical findings raise questions about the validity of proletarianization thesis, or at least the extent to which social workers accept it. It should be remembered, however, that the empirical shifts we have described are subtle and likely to be profoundly affected by future historical, political, and economic changes external to social work. Irrespective of which, if any, of these models ultimately prevails, the future shape of social work as an institution involves some difficult and important choices for all social workers.

THE FUTURE OF SOCIAL WORKER ACTIVISM

In contrast to the issue of professionalization, it is somewhat easier to extrapolate from our findings to the future shape of activism. Comparisons between the sixties and the eighties social workers show that they appear to be more rather than less involved in institutionalized forms of social action and electoral activism and less involved in protest in the latter period. It is difficult to say whether this is a consequence of slightly greater institutional professionalization or the decline of "oppositional activism" (Wagner 1987:331–376) in the society at large. Nevertheless, it is clear that differences in individual social worker professionalization are not associated with less participation in protest.

On the other hand, individual involvement in the occupation is positively associated with involvement in institutionalized forms of activism such as visiting public officials, participating in a social action committee of NASW, and the like.

Although social workers in the eighties were increasingly involved in electoral activism, a more radical interpretation of the political significance of this behavior has been suggested by Piven and Cloward. Like Jesse Jackson, they suggest that institutionally legitimated efforts to get the poor to register and vote are more disruptive to the political *status quo* than previously thought (Wills 1988).

Amidei (1987:2) nevertheless argues that there is "growing evidence of a new spirit of activism and politically conscious efforts on behalf of vulnerable people." She characterizes "1980s style activism" as spread out over many issues in which activists tend to utilize consensus strategies in the political arena rather than mass demonstrations or lawsuits. The social workers in 1984 seemed to have been highly involved in "1980s style activism."

The image of professionalization alongside of partisan political activism advocated by Bertha Reynolds seems to aptly portray contemporary social work. At the same time many social workers seem to have taken up Edith Abbott's notion of the obligation of social workers to improve the professional image and competitive position of social work. They are active in working for the licensing of social work and against the reclassification of social work jobs. Both of these sets of activities are consistent with two of the goals of NASW for 1988–1991: (1) "to promote the strength, unity, and recognition of the social work profession and acceptance and utilization of its standards," (2) "to promote and advance sound public policies and programs aimed at human need and improved quality of life" (NASW Newsletter 1988:4).

These findings suggest that future social worker activism will be positively rather than negatively associated with professionalization. However, the direction this activism will take is likely to be institutionally channeled.

As for social workers' future involvement in protest or oppositional activism, we would predict that historical movements external to social work and the background characteristics and related ideologies that future cohorts of social workers bring to the field will have more of an impact than will increasing professionalization.

The Future of Research on Social Work Professionalization and Activism

In 1983, Freidson suggested a new direction for the sociology of occupations and professions that seems to hold promise for future social work research as well. He argued that since many occupations do not attain the characteristics of the ideal professional model, "the whole rich variety is reduced to being merely non-professions, defined negatively and emptily as lacking professional characteristics" (p. 32). His strategy is to develop a more general, abstract theory of occupations that would include all occupations.

The theory of professions would no longer serve the function of ordering all occupations by professional ranking. Instead, it would develop a better means of understanding the complex, changing phenomena of professionalization. He (1983:33) stated that "the task for a theory of professions would be to document the untidiness and inconsistency of the empirical phenomenon and to explain its character in those countries where it exists."

He called for researchers to do case studies to analyze in detail all occupations called professions, including those occupations that label themselves as professions and do not receive public recognition. The ultimate goal is to establish bases for comparing occupations. Freidson's (1983:34–35) approach breaks with past research on the professions by its emphasis on the special characteristics of occupations rather than focusing on the extent to which they conform with the professional model of the established professions. In this way, new models of professions and professionalization may emerge that are more viable for all occupational groups.

Future social work researchers may follow Friedson's suggestion and devote themselves to research on the unique characteristics of social work as an occupation: that we entail continuing study of trends in social work professionalization and activism as well as historical and qualitative research on the symbolic meanings and interpretations of these trends.

Mintzberg's (1979) work on different types of organizational configurations also has implications for developing new models of professionalization. He poses a challenge to the notions that the true professional is an autonomous practitioner and that work in a bureaucratic organization is in conflict with attaining autonomy. Synthesizing the findings of previous empirical research on organizations, he proposed a new way to categorize organizations. Each type is a result of forces and conditions that favor a different coordinating mechanism being dominant, a different part of the organization being important, and a different type of decentralized decision making being used (1979:300–301).

The machine and professional bureaucracies seem to be the types most descriptive of the organizational contexts in which social workers are employed. The conditions that favor a machine bureaucracy are routine, simple, and repetitive work and work processes which are highly standardized (1979:315). It has the characteristics of the Weberian bureaucracy (e.g., reliance on hierarchical authority).

In the proletarianization literature, social workers have primarily been depicted as working in machine bureaucracies, and yet this type of organization would seem to best describe only those social workers working in larger bureaucracies with an emphasis on control, such as public welfare.

Alternatively, Mintzberg (1979:366) characterized professional bureaucracies as emphasizing the power of expertise of the professionals who draw on standards from outside the organization (1979:351). This organizational type has the structure of a rational bureaucracy and yet, the professionals control their own work. In contrast with the proletarianization theorists, Mintzberg regarded social work agencies as an example of professional bureaucracies. This type of organization is likely to characterize those social workers who are employed in agencies dominated by professional social workers (e.g., family service, child guidance).

Mintzberg (1979:474–475) also suggested that the organizational types may be used to describe hybrid organizations. For example, professional bureaucracies may take on certain characteristics of machine bureaucracies because of outside forces (e.g., government) exerting control.

Many scholars in the sociology of occupations and professions have ignored the variety of organizational contexts in which professionals work. They have generally viewed professionals as working in non-bureaucratic organizations (e.g., private practice) and aspiring professionals as employed in machine-type bureaucracies. Mintzberg provided a range of possible organizational configurations in which professionals and aspiring professionals may work (e.g., professional bureaucracy, machine bureaucracy, hybrid organizations) which can serve as a frame of reference for research to discover real-world structures. His organizational types can be used as theories to be empirically tested to develop a better means of understanding the complex phenomena of bureaucracy and to develop new models of professionalization on the basis of unique and common characteristics of occupations.

Future social work researchers may follow Mintzberg's lead and more effectively describe the structural characteristics of the organizations in which social workers are employed, the organization of their work, and the impact that these organizational factors have on social workers' professional and political consciousness.

Forsyth and Danisiewicz (1985:66) suggested that the primary differences among occupations claiming to be professions are due to the power profile exhibited by the members—autonomy from client and from workplace. They (1985:72) found that the power profiles of student aspirants to traditional professions (medicine, law) differed from those of the student aspirants to semi-professions (e.g., social work, nursing) "in predictable and patterned ways." Their findings suggest the utility of future social work researchers' surveying the perceptions of autonomy of social work practitioners and those from other occupations to determine if the results of their study are borne out by the perceptions of practitioners rather than the anticipations of students. In addition, samples taken from different social work agencies and from different segments within social work could shed more light on the proletarianization thesis and on issues of comparative professionalization of social work segments.

A final possible strategy for conducting future research on professionalization may be to move away from a broad conceptualization of professionalization and focus on single dimensions in relation to a wide range of workers' behaviors or of characteristics of the organizations they occupy (Wilson, Voth, and Hudson 1980). Support for this strategy is found in the present study which showed that the single dimensions of participation in

the profession and
predictive

B. *Index of Professional Participation**

ITEM: Please indicate the nature of your participation in the National Association of Social Workers (national chapter). (NA and "Member" = 1. "Take active part in affairs" = 2. "Hold office in" = 3.)

ITEM: Please indicate the nature of your participation in the National Association of Social Workers (local chapter). (Coded as item above.)

ITEM: Please indicate the number of times you have read a paper before a professional group. (NA and "Never" = 0, "Once" = 1, "2 or 3 Times" = 2, "4 or 5 Times" and "Over 5 Times" = 3.)

ITEM: Please indicate the number of times you have had a paper or article published in a professional journal. (Coded as item above.)

ITEM: Please indicate the number of social work or related conferences you have attended in the past year. (Coded as item above.)

ITEM: Please indicate the thoroughness with which you read professional journals. ("Read none regularly" = 0, "O through them" = 1, "Partial reading" = 2, "Th reading" = 3.)

Individual item scores were summed and trichot as follows:

Category	Raw Score
Low	0 – 5
Medium	6 – 7
High	8 – 18

ITEM: Please indicate the nature of your participatio

*Reeser added this item—Please indicate the nature of your participation
Association of Social Workers (state).

C. *Index of Professionalism**

ITEM: In order to be effective, a social worker m control over his or her emotions. ("Strong 7, "2" = 6, "3" = 5, "4" and NA = 4, " "Strongly Disagree—7" = 1.)

n
al

by
stud
as we
be est
propose
   More
fered in
group are
potheses t
cally validat
in the contin

ITEM: The public expression of political values should always be avoided by social workers in their professional roles. (Coded as item above.)

ITEM: Social workers should at all times avoid political discussions with their clients or client groups. (Coded as item above.)

ITEM: There is generally a great difference between a low-income client's view of the causes of his problem, and the real reason for his problem.** (Coded as item above.)

ITEM: Social workers should at all times maintain a restrained and dignified manner with clients. (Coded as item above.)

Individual item scores were summed and trichotomized as follows:

Category	Raw Score
Low	0 – 15
Medium	16 – 20
High	21 – 35

*Reeser added this item—Persons who violate professional standards should be judged only by their professional peers. (Coded as items above.)

**Reeser did not include this item in her index.

D. *Index of Autonomy**

ITEM: There is little autonomy in my work. ("Strongly Agree—7" = 1; "Moderately Agree—6" = 2; "Mildly Agree—5" = 3; "Neutral" = 4; "Mildly Disagree—3" = 5; "Moderately Disagree—2" = 6; "Strongly Disagree—1" = 7.)

ITEM: When problems arise at work there is little opportunity to implement my own ideas. (Coded as item above.)

ITEM: Going through the proper channels at all times is constantly stressed in my organization. (Seven-point scale, "Strongly Agree"—7 to "Strongly Disagree"—1.)

ITEM: It seems as though there is a rule for everything in my organization. (Coded as item above.)

ITEM: Any decision I make at work has to have the supervisor's approval. (Coded as item above.)

Individual item scores were summed and trichotomized as follows:

Category	Raw Score
Low	0 – 19
Medium	20 – 23
High	24 – 28

*NAs were excluded from the index.

II. *Indices of Social Activism*

   A. *Index of Commitment to Activist Goals**

      ITEM: Some social workers feel that social work should help the individual find a mode of adaptation to the world around him/her and others feel that emphasis should be placed on societal change. While both approaches are valuable and not necessarily in conflict with each other, which would *you* favor if you had to make a choice? (Individual adaptation = 1; Societal change = 2.)

      ITEM: Choose one. (1) Social work should devote equal attention and equal resources to all social class groupings. (2) Social work should devote most of its attention and resources to the problems of the poor.

      Scoring: Those scoring high would answer 2 on the first item and 2 on the second item. Any other combination of items is scored as low.

Category	Raw Score
Low	0 – 3
High	4

*NAs were excluded from the index.

   B. *Index of Public Welfare Conflict Approval**

      ITEM: Suppose a group of PROFESSIONAL SOCIAL WORKERS, acting as representatives of the profession, felt it would be desirable to get MORE GOVERNMENT-SPONSORED PROGRAMS TO HELP PUBLIC WELFARE RECIPIENTS. While you may or may not agree that this goal is desirable, please indicate . . . whether you would approve or disapprove the group's taking EACH of the following social actions.

ITEM: Inform public welfare recipients of their rights and encourage them to file complaints about inadequate welfare provisions through the Department of Welfare. ("Strongly approve—1, 2, 3" = 1; "4, 5, 6, Strongly Disapprove—7," NA = 0.)

ITEM: Openly campaign for political candidates or work through political parties which favor more governmental programs for welfare recipients. (Coded as item above.)

ITEM: Offer support to local community action groups that request help in organizing welfare recipients to conduct protest demonstrations at the Department of Welfare. (Coded as item above.)

ITEM: Actively organize welfare recipients to conduct protest demonstrations at the Department of Welfare. (Coded as item above.)

Individual item scores were summed and dichotomized as follows:

Category	*Number of Items* *Approved*
Low	0 – 2
High	3 – 4

*These items also form a Guttman Scale (in the order presented) with a coefficient of reproducibility of .96. Since there are only four items, however, it was felt that a simple dichotomy based on the number of conflict strategies approved was the most appropriate way to construct the index.

C. *Indices of Activist Behavior*

1. *Index of Institutionalized Social Action Behavior**

ITEM: Respondent indicates whether he/she has taken any of the following institutionalized social actions within the past year.

ITEM: Testified before public bodies.** ("Yes" = 1, "No," NA = 0.)

ITEM: Visited a public official with a group. (Coded as item above.)

ITEM: Gave service to an NASW committee involved in social action. (Coded as item above.)

ITEM: Gave service to an agency committee involved in social action. (Coded as item above.)

ITEM: Participated in social work lobbying for legislation.**
(Coded as item above.)

ITEM: Made efforts in a professional capacity to influence opinion among the general public (e.g., public speaking,
preparation of informational material, etc.). (Coded as
item above.)

Individual item scores were summed and dichotomized as follows:

Category	Number of Actions Taken
Low	0
High	1 – 6

*Reeser added these items: "Help in a fund-raising campaign" (coded as items above);
"Participate in a grass roots organization" (coded as items above).

**Reeser did not include this item in her index.

2. *Index of Noninstitutionalized Social Action Behavior**

ITEM: Respondent indicates whether he/she has taken any of
the following noninstitutionalized social actions within
the past year.

ITEM: Joined a protest parade. ("Yes" = 1; "No," NA = 0.)

ITEM: Engaged in civil disobedience. (Coded as item above.)

ITEM: Picketed.** (Coded as item above.)

ITEM: Gave service to social work groups primarily concerned
with direct action (e.g., Social Workers for Peaceful
Negotiation, Social Workers for Civil Rights Action,
etc.).** (Coded as item above.)

Individual item scores were summed and dichotomized as follows:

	Category	Number of Actions Taken
Epstein:	Low	0
	High	1 – 4
Reeser:	Low	0
	High	1 – 3

*Reeser added this item: "Organize a demonstration or protest."

**Reeser did not include this item in her index.

3. *Index of Electoral Social Action Behavior**
   Respondent indicates whether he/she has done any of the following activities in an election campaign in the past five years.
   ITEM: Contribute money to a political campaign. ("Yes" = 2; "No" = 1.)
   ITEM: Sign letters or petitions supporting a candidate. (Coded as item above.)
   ITEM: Attend public rallies or meetings. (Coded as item above.)
   Individual item scores were summed and trichotomized as follows:

Category	Raw Score
Low	0 – 3
Medium	4 – 5
High	6

*NAs were excluded frcm the index.

4. *Index of Professional Social Action Behavior*
   Respondent indicates whether he/she has done any of the following professional activities in the past year.
   ITEM: Participate in social work lobbying for legislation. ("Frequently" = 2; "Occasionally" = 1; "Not at all," NA = 0.)
   ITEM: Work to get licensing passed in your state. (Coded as item above.)
   ITEM: Work against the declassification of social work. (Coded as item above.)
   Individual item scores were summed and dichotomized as follows:

Category	Raw Score
Low	0
High	1 – 6

NOTES

CHAPTER 1

1. The items concerning approval of strategies to change the public welfare system are dealt with descriptively in this section of the chapter. Later on in this chapter, practice groups are compared on their scores on a public welfare conflict index. Epstein (1969) constructed this index using items concerning approval of institutionalized and noninstitutionalized conflict strategies. Consensus strategies were excluded from the index because the majority of respondents endorsed these strategies.

CHAPTER 2

1. Although the ratio of men to women in social work has been fairly consistent, there has been an increase in female and a decrease in male membership. During the period 1972 to 1982 female membership increased from 59 to 73 percent, while male membership decreased from 41 to 27 percent (Hopps and Pinderhughes 1987:357).

2. Although both samples contained sufficient numbers of Black Catholics to treat them and Black Protestants as separate groups, the social action attitudes and behaviors of these two groups were virtually identical within each sample. Consequently, Black Catholics and Black Protestants are presented in our table as one group. These findings support the contention that for Blacks race is more salient than religious affiliation in shaping their social activism.

CHAPTER 3

1. In general, the Scott Professional Role Orientation index did not indicate significant differences between the 1968 and 1984 samples. However, we found that social workers in 1984 were significantly more likely than those in 1968 to choose colleagues in the agency as a source of professional stimulation ($p < .01$).

2. Wilensky's scoring system and cutoff points were used in making these comparisons. However, since our samples were drawn from different universes, at different points in time, using different assumptions, etc., and since ours was a self-administered version of Wilensky's interview items, tests of statistical significance were not applied to the comparisons of Wilensky's and our data.

3. We chose the Billingsley Role Orientation index as our reference group measure and will continue to do so for the remainder of the book. Although each professional role orientation index has its flaws, the Billingsley index is the only one developed and tested with master's degree social workers.

CHAPTER 4

1. Only the more widely used Billingsley Role Orientation measure is used to assess respondents' reference groups. Nevertheless, the findings using the other measures were quite similar to those found using the Billingsley measure.

2. Epstein (1968) and Reeser (1986) used a few different items in their respective indices of values of professionalism. Reeser did not include social distance from the poor and Epstein did not include professional self-regulation. In all other respects, their scales were identical.

3. Because of the relatively small number of group workers and community organizers in the sample, representatives of these two segments were combined for analysis of noncaseworkers.

REFERENCES _____

Abzug, Bella S., and Mim Kelber. 1984. *Gender Gap: Bella Abzug's Guide to Political Power for American Women*. Boston: Houghton Mifflin Company.

Alexander, Chauncey A. 1982. "Professional social workers and political responsibility." In Maryann Mahaffey and John W. Hanks, eds., *Practical Politics: Social Work and Political Responsibility*, pp. 15–31. Maryland: National Association of Social Workers.

Alexander, Leslie B. 1980. "Professionalization and unionization: compatible after all." *Social Work* 25:474–484.

Almond, Gabriel A., and Sidney Verba. 1965. *The Civic Culture*. Boston: Little, Brown and Company.

Alston, Jon, and Imogene K. Dean. 1972. "Socio-economic factors associated with attitudes toward welfare recipients and the causes of poverty." *Social Service Review* 46:13–23.

Amidei, Nancy. 1978. "The new activism picks up steam." *Public Welfare* 45:21–26.

Antunes, George, and Charles M. Gortz. 1975. "Ethnicity and participation: a study of Mexican-Americans, Blacks, and whites." *American Journal of Sociology* 80:1192–1211.

Austin, David M. 1985. "Historical perspectives on contemporary social work." *The Urban and Social Change Review* 18:16–18.

Babchuk, Nicholas, and Ralph V. Thompson. 1962. "The voluntary associations of Negroes." *American Sociological Review* 27:647–655.

Baker, Sally Hillsman. 1978. "Women in blue-collar and service occupations." In Ann Stromberg and Shirley Harkess, eds., *Women Working: Theories and Facts in Perspective*, pp. 339–376. Palo Alto, CA: Mayfield.

Baxter, Sandra, and Marjorie Lansing. 1983. *Women and Politics*. Ann Arbor: The University of Michigan Press.

Beck, Bertram M. 1977. "Professional associations: NASW." *Encyclopedia of Social Work* 1:1084–1093.

Benguigui, Georges. 1967. "La professionalisation des cadres dans l'industrie." *Sociologie du Travail* 8:134–143.

Benson, John M. 1981. "The polls: a rebirth of religion?" *Public Opinion Quarterly* 45:576–585.

Benthrup, Walter C. 1964. "The professions and the means test." *Social Work* 9:10–17.

Berelson, Bernard R., Paul F. Lazarsfeld, and William N. McPhee. 1954. *Voting.* Chicago: University of Chicago Press.

Bielby, William T., and James N. Baron. 1984. "A woman's place is with other women: sex segregation within organizations." In Barbara F. Reskin, ed., *Sex Segregation in the Workplace: Trends, Explanations, Remedies,* pp. 27–55. Washington, D.C.: National Academy Press.

Billingsley, Andrew. 1964a. "Bureaucratic and professional orientation patterns in social casework." *Social Service Review* 4:400–407.

—— 1964b. *The Role of the Social Worker in a Child Protective Agency: A Comparative Analysis.* Boston: Society for the Prevention of Cruelty to Children.

Billups, James O. 1984. "Unifying social work: importance of center-moving ideas. *Social Work,* 29:173–180.

Binstock, Robert H. 1974. "Aging and the future of American politics." *The Annals of the American Academy of Political and Social Science,* 415:199–212.

—— 1981. "Interest group liberalism and the politics of aging." In Robert B. Hudson, ed., *The Aging in Politics: Process and Policy,* pp. 47–73. Springfield, IL: Charles C. Thomas.

Bisno, Herbert. 1952. *The Philosophy of Social Work.* Washington: Public Affairs Press.

—— 1956. "How social will social work be?" *Social Work* 1:12–18.

Blau, Francine O. 1978. "The data on women workers, past, present, and future." In Ann Stromberg and Shirley Harkess, eds., *Women Workers: Theories and Facts in Perspective,* pp. 29–62. Palo Alto, CA: Mayfield.

Borenzweig, Herman. 1971. "Social work and psychoanalytic theory: a historical analysis." *Social Work* 16:7–16.

Bourque, Susan, and Jean Grossholtz. 1974. "Politics as an unnatural practice: political science looks at female participation." *Politics and Society,* 4:225–266.

Brager, George A., and Francis P. Purcell, eds. 1967. *Community Action Against Poverty.* New Haven: College and University Press.

Briar, Scott. 1987. "Direct practice: trends and issues." *Encyclopedia of Social Work* 1:393–398.

Brilland, Donald. 1987. "History and evolution of social work practice." *Encyclopedia of Social Work* 1:739–753.

Bucher, Rue, and Anselm Strauss. 1961. "Professions in process." *American Journal of Sociology,* 66: 325–334.

Burghardt, Steve. 1982. *The Other Side of Organizing.* Cambridge, MA: Schenkman Publishing Company.

Bush, Rod. 1984. *The New Black Vote.* San Francisco: Synthesis Publications.

Campbell, Angus, Philip E. Converse, Warren E. Miller, and Donald E. Stokes. 1964. *The American Voter: An Abridgement.* New York: John Wiley.

Caplow, Theodore. 1954. *The Sociology of Work.* Minneapolis University of Minnesota Press.

Carr-Saunders, A. M. 1965. "Metropolitan conditions and traditional professional relationships." In Robert M. Fisher, ed., *The Metropolis in Modern Life,* pp. 279–287. Garden City, NY: Doubleday and Co.

Carr-Saunders, A. M., and P. A. Wilson. 1933. *The Professions.* Oxford, England: Clarendon Press.

Cavanaugh, Thomas G. 1985. *Inside Black America: The Message of the Black Vote in the 1984 Elections.* Washington, D.C.: Joint Center for Political Studies, Inc.

Centers, Richard. 1961. *The Psychology of Social Classes.* New York: Russell and Russell.

Chess, Wayne A., Julia M. Norlin, and Srinika Jayaratne. 1983. *On the Privatization of Social Work: Results of a National Survey.* Unpublished paper, University of Oklahoma, School of Social Work.

Cloward, Richard A., and Irwin Epstein. 1965. "Private social welfare's disengagement from the poor: the case of private family adjustment agencies." *Proceedings of the Annual Social Work Day Institute.* Buffalo: State University of Buffalo.

Cohen, Michael. 1966. "The emergence of private practice in social work." *Social Problems,* 14:84–93.

Cooper, Shirley. 1977. "Social work: a dissenting profession." *Social Work,* 22:360–367.

Cummings, Joan E. 1980. "Sexism in social work: some thoughts on strategy for structural change." *Catalyst* 9:6–32.

Cyrns, Arthur. 1977. "Social work education and student ideology: a multivariate study of professional socialization." *Journal of Education for Social Work* 13:44–51.

Dawson, Richard E., and Kenneth Prewitt. 1969. *Political Socialization.* Boston: Little, Brown and Company.

Dean, Walter R., Jr. 1977. "Back to activism." *Social Work,* 22:369–373.

Divers, Arthur Jesse. 1980. "An analysis of the relationship of teacher job satisfaction and teacher union activism in the Detroit public school system." Ph.D. dissertation, University of Michigan. In *Dissertation Abstracts International,* Vol. 41, Sec. A., p. 3795.

Dressel, Paula, Michelle Waters, Mike Sweat, et. al. 1988. "Deprofessionalization, proletarianization, and social welfare work." *Journal of Sociology and Social Welfare* 15:113–131.

Durkheim, Emile. 1933. *The Division of Labor in Society.* 2d ed. New York: Macmillan Publishing Co., Inc., Free Press Paperback.

Dyer, Preston M. 1977. "How professional is the B.S.W. worker?" *Social Work,* 22:487–492.

Eaton, Joseph W. 1956. "Whence and whither social work?: a sociological analysis." *Social Work,* January 1956, pp. 11–26.

Eisenger, Peter K. 1974. "Racial differences in protest participation." *American Political Science Review* 68:592–606.

Engel, Gloria V. 1970. "Professional autonomy and bureaucratic organization. *Administrative Science Quarterly,* 10:12–21.

Epstein, Cynthia F. 1981. *Women in Law.* New York: Anchor Books.

Epstein, Irwin. 1969. "Professionalization and social-work activism." Ph.D. dissertation, Columbia University.

Epstein, Irwin, and Kayla Conrad. 1978. "The empirical limits of professionalization." In Rosemary G. Sarri and Yeheskel Hasenfeld, eds., *The Management of Human Services,* pp. 163–183. New York: Columbia University Press.

Etzioni, Amitai. 1964. *Modern Organizations.* Englewood Cliffs, NJ: Prentice-Hall.

—— 1969. *The Semi-Professions and Their Organization.* New York: Free Press.

Farley, Reynolds. 1984. *Blacks and Whites: Narrowing the Gap?* Cambridge, MA: Harvard University Press.

Feagin, Joe R. 1975. *Subordinating the Poor: Welfare and American Beliefs.* Englewood Cliffs, New Jersey: Prentice-Hall, Inc.

Flexner, Abraham. 1915. "Is social work a profession?" In *Proceedings of the National Conference of Charities and Corrections*, pp. 576-590. Chicago.

Forsyth, Patrick B. and Thomas J. Danisiewicz. 1985. "Toward a theory of professionalization." *Work and Occupations*, 12:59–75.

Fox, Mary Frank. 1987. "Women in the labor force: position, plight, prospects." In Josefina Figueira-McDonough and Rosemary Sarri, eds., *The Trapped Woman: Catch 22 in Deviance and Control*, pp. 197–215. Newbury Park: Sage Publications.

Fox, William S., and Michael H. Wince. 1976. "The structure and determinants of occupational militancy among public school teachers." *Industrial and Labor Relations Review*, 30:47–58.

Freidson, Eliot. 1970. *Professional Dominance.* Chicago: Aldine Publishing Company.

—— 1973. "Professions and the occupational principle." In Eliot Freidson, ed., *The Professions and Their Prospects*, pp. 19–38. Beverly Hills, California: Sage Publications.

—— 1983. "The theory of professions: state of the art." In Robert Dingwell and Philip Lewis, eds., The Sociology of the Professions: Lawyers, Doctors and Others, pp. 19–37. London: The Macmillan Press.

—— 1984. "The changing nature of professional control." *Annual Review of Sociology*, 10:1–20.

Freidson, Eliot, and Rhea Buford. 1965. "Knowledge and judgement in professional evaluations." *Administrative Science Quarterly* 10:107–124.

Galper, Jeffry. 1975. *The Politics of Social Services.* Englewood Cliffs, NJ: Prentice-Hall, Inc.

Gelb, Joyce, and Marian Lief Palley. 1982. *Women and Public Policies.* Princeton, NJ: Princeton University Press.

Germain, Carol. 1973. "An ecological perspective in casework practice." *Social Casework*, 54:323–330.

Ghere, Richard K. 1981. "Effects of service delivery variations on administration of municipal human service agencies: the contract approach versus agency implementation." *Administration in Social Work* 5:65–78.

Glenn, Norval D. 1981. "Aging and conservatism." In Robert B. Hudson, ed., *The Aging in Politics: Process and Policy*, pp. 19–29. Springfield, IL: Charles C. Thomas.

Glenn, Norval D., and M. Grimes. 1968. "Aging, voting, and political interest." *American Sociological Review*, 33:563–575.

Goode, William J. 1957. "Community within a community: the professions." *American Sociological Review*, 22:194–200.

—— 1969. "The theoretical limits of professionalization." In Amitai Etzioni, ed., *The Semi-Professions and Their Organization*, pp. 266–313. New York: The Free Press.

Gouldner, Alvin W. 1958. "Cosmopolitans and locals: toward an analysis of latent social roles—I. *Administrative Science Quarterly*, 2:281–306.

—— 1961. "Metaphysical pathos and the theory of bureaucracy." In Amitai Etzioni, ed., *Complex Organizations*, pp. 71–82. New York: Holt, Rinehart and Winston.

Greenwood, Ernest. 1957. "Attributes of a profession." *Social Work,* 2:44–55.

Grønbjerg, Kristen A., David Street, and Gerald D. Suttles. 1978. *Poverty and Social Change.* Chicago: The University of Chicago Press.

Hage, Jerald and Michael Aiken. 1967. "Program change and organizational properties." *American Journal of Sociology,* 72:503–519.

Hall, Richard H. 1968. "Professionalization and bureaucratization." *American Sociological Review,* 33:92–103.

Halmos, Paul. 1970. *The Personal Service Society.* New York: Schocken Books.

Hamilton, Richard F. 1966. "The marginal middle-class: a reconsideration." *American Sociological Review* 31:192–199.

Hanna, Herbert W. 1975. "The associations between social work value orientations, social work education, professional attitudes and organizational structure with the job satisfaction of social workers." Ph.D. dissertation, Ohio State University.

Haug, Marie R. 1975. "The deprofessionalization of everyone?" *Sociological Focus,* 8:197–213.

Haynes, Karen S., and James S. Mickelson. 1986. *Affecting Change: Social Workers in the Political Arena.* New York: Longman Inc.

Heffernan, Joseph W. 1964. "Political activity and social work executives." *Social Work,* 9:18–23.

Hendrickson, Robert M., and Leland J. Axelson. 1985. "Middle-class attitudes toward the poor: are they changing?" *Social Service Review* 59:295–304.

Heraud, Brian F. 1973. "Professionalism, radicalism, and social change." In Paul Halmos, ed., *Professionalisation and Social Change,* pp. 85–101. Keele: The University of Keele, The Sociological Review Monograph 20.

Herberg, Will. 1960. *Protestant-Catholic-Jew.* New York: Doubleday Anchor Books.

Hollingshead, August B. 1965. "Two-factor index of social position." Unpublished paper, New Haven.

Hopps, June Gary, and Elaine B. Pinderhughes. 1987. "Profession of social work: contemporary characteristics." *Encyclopedia of Social Work* 2:351–366.

Howe, Elizabeth. 1980. "Public professions and the private model of professionalism." *Social Work,* 25:174–190.

Hughes, Everett C. 1958. *Men and Their Work.* Glencoe, IL: Free Press.

Hyman, Herbert. 1959. *Political Socialization.* Glencoe, IL: Free Press.

Hyman, Herbert H., and Charles R. Wright. 1971. "Trends in voluntary association membership of American adults: replication based on secondary analysis of national sample surveys." *American Sociological Review* 36:191–206.

Iglehart, Alfreda P. 1979. *Married Women and Work.* Lexington, MA: D. C. Heath and Company.

Illich, Ivan. 1976. *Limits to Medicine.* London: Marion Boyars.

Isaac, Larry, Elizabeth Mutran, and Sheldon Stryker. 1980. "Political protest orientations among Black and white adults." *American Sociological Review* 45:191–213.

Isaacs, Stephen D. 1974. *Jews and American Politics.* New York: Doubleday and Company, Inc.

Jennings, James. 1984. "Blacks and progressive politics." In Rod Bush, ed., *The New Black Vote,* pp. 199–302. San Francisco: Synthesis Publications.

Johnson, Terence J. 1972. *Professions and Power.* London: Macmillan.

Jones, Rochelle. 1977. *The Other Generation: The New Power of Older People.* Englewood Cliffs, NJ: Prentice-Hall, Inc.

Kadushin, Alfred. 1959. "The knowledge base of social work. In Alfred J. Kahn, ed., *Issues in American Social Work,* pp. 53–58. New York: Columbia University Press.

Kahn, Alfred J. 1954. "The nature of social work knowledge." In Cora Kasius, ed., *New Directions in Social Work,* pp. 194–214. New York: Harper and Brothers.

Kirkpatrick, Jeane J. 1974. *Political Woman.* New York: Basic Books, Inc.

Klobus-Edwards, Patricia, John N. Edwards, and David Klemmock. 1978. "Differences in social participation: Blacks and whites." *Social Forces* 56:1035–1071.

Knoke, David. 1974. "Religion, stratification, and politics America in the 1960s." *American Journal of Political Science,* 18:331–345.

Kolker, Ann. 1983. "Women lobbyists." In Irene Tinker, ed., *Women in Washington: Advocates for Public Policy,* pp. 209–225. Beverly Hills: Sage Publications.

Kravetz, Diane. 1976. "Sexism in a woman's profession." *Social Work* 21:421.

—— 1982. "An overview of content on women for the social work curriculum." *Journal of Education for Social Work* 18:42–49.

Landecker, Werner S. 1951. "Types of integration and their measurement." *American Journal of Sociology* 56:332–340.

Langerock, Hubert. 1915. "Professionalism: a study in professional deformation." *American Journal of Sociology* 20:30–44.

Larson, Magali Sarfati. 1977. *The Rise of Professionalism.* Berkeley, CA: University of California Press.

Le Guin, Ursula K. "Loon woman in the long ago." (Review of John Bierhorst's *The Mythology of North America.) The New York Times Book Review.* September 1, 1985:7.

Lee, Porter R. 1929. "Social work: cause and function." In *National Conference on Social Work Proceedings,* pp. 3–20. Chicago: University of Chicago Press.

Leighninger, Leslie. 1986. "Bertha Reynolds and Edith Abbott: contrasting images of professionalism in social work." *Smith College Studies in Social Work* 56:111–121.

Leighninger, Leslie. 1978. "Professionalism and social work education: substance and structure." *Journal of Sociology and Social Welfare* 5:188–213.

Lenski, Gerhard. 1961. *The Religious Factor.* New York: Doubleday and Company, Inc.

Leuchtenburg, William E. 1958. *The Perils of Prosperity 1914–1932.* Chicago: The University of Chicago Press.

—— 1963. *Franklin D. Roosevelt and the New Deal 1932–1940.* New York: Harper and Row Publishers.

Levenstein, Sidney. 1964. *Private Practice in Social Casework.* New York: Columbia University Press.

Lightman, Ernie S. 1982. "Professionalization, bureaucratization, and unionization in social work." *Social Service Review* 56:130–143.

Lindeman, Edward C. 1952. "Introduction." In Herbert Bisno *The Philosophy of Social Work,* pp. v–vi. Washington: Public Affairs Press.

Lipset, Seymour Martin. 1968. *Revolution and Counterrevolution.* New York: Basic Books, Inc.

Lipset, Seymour Martin, and Reinhard Bendix. 1960. *Social Mobility in Industrial Society.* Berkeley and Los Angeles: University of California Press.

Lipsky, Michael. 1980. *Street-Level Bureaucracy: Dilemmas of the Individual in Public Services.* New York: Russell Sage Foundation.

Loether, Herman J. and Donald G. McTavish. 1980. *Descriptive and Inferential Statistics: An Introduction.* Boston, MA: Allyn and Bacon, Inc.

Longres, John F., and Robert H. Bailey. 1979. "Men's issues and sexism: a journal review." *Social Work* 24:26–32.

Lopreato, Joseph. 1967. "Upward social mobility and political orientation." *American Sociological Review* 32:586–592.

Lubove, Roy. 1965. *The Professional Altruist.* Cambridge, M.A.: Harvard University Press.

MacRae, Robert H. 1966. "Social work and social action." *Social Service Review* 40:1–7.

Mahler, Ronnie. 1982. "Baccalaureate social work graduates: reflection on employment, professional identification, and education preparedness." *Journal of Education for Social Work* 18:80–85.

Mannheim, Karl. 1936. *Ideology and Utopia.* New York: Harvest Books.

March, James G., and Herbert A. Simon. 1958. *Organizations.* New York: John Wiley and Sons.

Marshall, T. H. 1965. "The recent history of professionalism in relation to social structure and social policy." In T. H. Marshall, ed., *Class Citizenship and Social Development,* pp. 158-179. Garden City: Doubleday Anchor Books.

Martin, Lawrence Lee. 1985. "Purchase of service contracting under the social services block grant: an analysis of state systems." Ph.D. dissertation, Arizona State University.

McCann, Charles W., and Jane Park Cutler. 1979. "Ethics and the alleged unethical." *Social Work* 24:5–8.

Meyer, Carol H. 1980. "Issues for women in a 'woman's profession'." In Ann Weick and Susan T. Vandiver, eds., *Women, Power, and Change,* pp. 197–205. Washington, D.C.: National Association of Social Workers.

Middleman, Ruth R., and Gale Goldberg. 1987. "Social work practice with groups." *Encyclopedia of Social Work* 2:714–729.

Milbrath, Lester W. 1965. *Political Participation.* Chicago: Rand McNally.

Miller, Henry. 1981. "Dirty sheets: a multivariate analysis. *Social Work* 26:268–271.

Mills, C. Wright. 1953. *White Collar.* New York: Oxford University Press.

Minahan, Anne. 1981. "Purpose and objectives of social work revisited." *Social Work* 26:5–6.

Mintzberg, Henry. 1979. *The Structuring of Organizations.* Englewood Cliffs, NJ: Prentice-Hall.

Moynihan, Daniel P. 1965. "The professionalization of reform." *The Public Interest* 1:6–16.

Mueller, Candace P. 1978. "Purchase of service contracting from the viewpoint of the provider." In Kenneth R. Wedel, Arthur J. Katz, and Ann Weick, eds., *Proceedings of the National Institute on Purchase of Service Contracting,* pp. 46–54. New York: Praeger Publishers.

—— 1980. "Five years later—a look at title XX: the federal billion dollar social services fund." *The Grantsmanship Center News* 8:27–37, 56-58.

NASW News. October 1983. Vol. 28:7. "Mass of members at march."

NASW News. June 1985. Vol 30:6–7. "Trend toward licensure grows despite some vocal opposition."

NASW News. October 1985. Vol 30:17. "Leaders mark 30 years of studies by profession."

NASW News. May 1986. Vol. 31:1, 10. "Apartheid protested by NASW leaders."

NASW News. May 1986. Vol. 31:1, 30–31. "Public child welfare's crisis under scrutiny."

NASW Newsletter. Michigan Chapter. February 1988. Vol 12:4.

Nie, Norman H., Sidney Verba, and John R. Petrocik. 1979. *The Changing American Voter.* Cambridge, MA: Harvard University Press.

Papell, Catharine P., and Beulah Rothman. 1966. "Social group work models: possession and heritage." *Journal of Education for Social Work* 2:66–77.

Parsons, Talcott. 1958. "The professions and social structure" (1939). In Talcott Parsons, ed., *Essays in Sociological Theory,* rev. ed., pp. 34-50. Glencoe, IL: The Free Press.

—— 1964. *The Social System.* New York: Free Press Paperback.

Perlman, N., and J. A. Grune. 1980. "Preliminary memorandum on pay equity." Working Paper No. 2. Albany, NY: Center for Women in Government.

Piven, Frances Fox. 1966. "Participation of residents in neighborhood community action programs." *Social Work* 11:73–80.

Popple, Philip R. 1985. "The social work profession: a reconceptualization." *Social Service Review* 59:560–577.

Posey, Douglas P. 1978. "Personal and professional values among Colorado social workers." Ph.D. dissertation, University of Denver.

Potter, Sandra J. 1979. "Social workers, social activism and the community mental health center." Ph.D. dissertation, Western Michigan University.

Pratt, Henry J. 1974. "Old age organizations in national politics." *The Annals of the American Academy of Political and Social Science* 415:106–119.

Pray, Kenneth L. N. 1959. "Social work and social action." In Ernest B. Harper and Arthur Dunham, eds., *Community Organization in Action,* pp. 291-301. New York: Association Press.

Reeser, Linda C. 1986. "Professionalization and social activism." Ph.D. dissertation, Bryn Mawr College.

Rein, Martin. 1970. "Social work in search of a radical profession." *Social Work* 15:13–28.

Richan, Willard C., and Allan R. Mendelsohn. 1973. *Social Work: The Unloved Profession.* New York: New Viewpoints.

Roth, Julius. 1974. "Professionalism: the sociologist's decoy." *Sociology of Work and Occupations* 1:6–23.

Rubenstein, W. D. 1982. *The Left, the Right, and the Jews.* New York: Universe Books.

Rubin, Allen, Peter J. Johnson, and Kevin L. DeWeaver. 1986. "Direct practice interests of MSW students: changes from entry to graduation." *Journal of Education for Social Work* 22:98–108.

Sancier, Betty. 1980. "Beyond advocacy." In Ann Weick and Susan T. Vandiver, eds., *Women, Power and Change,* pp. 186–196. Washington, D.C.: National Association of Social Workers, Inc.

Schatzman, Leonard, and Anselm Strauss. 1966. "The sociology of psychiatry: a perspective and some organizing foci." *Social Problems* 14:3–16.

Schmidhauser, John R. 1970. "The elderly and politics." In Adeline M. Hoffman, ed., *The Daily Needs and Interests of Older People,* pp. 70–82. Springfield, IL: Charles C. Thomas.

Schorr, Alvin L. 1959. "The retreat to technician." *Social Work* 4:29–33.

Scott, W. Richard. 1965. "Reactions to supervision in a heteronomous professional organization." *Administrative Science Quarterly* 10:65–81

—— 1966. "Professionals in bureaucracies—areas of conflict." In Howard M. Vollmer and Donald L. Mills, eds., *Professionalization,* pp. 265–275. Englewood Cliffs, NJ: Prentice-Hall.

Shaffer, Gary L. 1979. "Labor relations and the unionization of professional social workers: a neglected area of social work education." *Journal of Education for Social Work* 15:80–86.

Shaw, Ian F. 1985 "A closed profession? recruitment to social work." *British Journal of Social Work* 15:261–279.

Simon, Bernece K. 1977. "Diversity and unity in the social work profession." *Social Work* 22:394-400.

Social Work. 1981. Vol 26:522–525. "Points and viewpoints."

Souflée, Federico, Jr. 1977. "Social work: the acquiescing profession." *Social Work* 22:419-421.

Spaulding, Charles B., Carl C. Hetrick, and Henry A. Turner. 1973. "Political activism and attitudes of academically affiliated sociologists." *Sociology and Social Research* 57:413–428.

Spaulding, Charles B., Henry A. Turner, and Charles G. McClintock. 1963. "Political orientations of academically affiliated sociologists." *Sociology and Social Research* 47:273–289.

Specht, Harry. 1972. "The deprofessionalization of social work." *Social Work* 17:3–15.

Statistical Abstract of the United States, 108th ed. 1988. Washington, D.C.: U. S. Bureau of the Census (1987).

Steele, Shelby. "Blinded by idealism." (Review of Jonathan Kaufman's *Broken Alliance: The Turbulent Times Between Blacks and Jews in America.*) *New York Times Book Review.* October 9, 1988:11.

Stewart, Robert P. 1981. "Watershed days: how will social work respond to the conservative revolution?" *Social Work* 26:271–273.

—— 1984. "From the president." *NASW News* 29:2.

Syrkin, Marie. 1980. *The State of the Jews.* Washington, D.C.: New Republic Books.

Thomson, Randall, and David Knoke. 1980. "Voluntary associations and voting turnout of American ethnoreligious groups." *Ethnicity* 7:56–69.

Thursz, Daniel. 1966. "Social action as a professional responsibility." *Social Work* 11: 12–21.

Tolman, Richard M., Donald D. Mowry, Linda E. Jones, and John Brekke. 1986. "Developing a profeminist commitment among men in social work." In Nan VanDenBergh and Lynn B. Cooper, eds., *Feminist Visions for Social Work,* pp. 61–79. Silver Spring, Maryland: National Association of Social Workers.

Toren, Nina. 1972. *Social Work: The Case of a Semi-Profession.* Beverly Hills, CA: Sage Publications.

Trattner, Walter I. 1974. *From Poor Law to Welfare State: A History of Social Welfare in America.* New York: The Free Press.

Treiman, Donald J., and Heidi I. Hartmann. 1981. *Women, Work, and Wages: Equal Pay for Jobs of Equal Value.* Washington, D.C.: National Academy Press.

Tropp, Emanuel. 1971. "Social group work: the developmental approach." *Encyclopedia of Social Work* 2:1246–1252.

Tutu, Bishop Desmond. "Mythology." (Review of Leonard Thompson's *The Political Mythology of Apartheid.*) *The New York Review of Books.* September 26, 1985:2–3.

Urban and Social Change Review, The. 1985. Vol. 18, Summer and Winter. "Has social work abandoned social welfare?"

Vandiver, Susan T. 1980. "A herstory of women in social work." In Elaine Norman and Ailine Mancuso, eds., *Women's Issues and Social Work Practice*, pp. 21–38. Itasca, IL: F. E. Peacock Publishers.

Verba, Sidney, and Norman H. Nie. 1981. "Participation and the life-cycle." In Robert B. Hudson, ed., *The Aging in Politics: Process and Policy*, pp. 8–18. Sprringfield, IL: Charles C. Thomas.

Vinter, Robert D. 1959. "The social structure of service. ' In Alfred J. Kahn, ed., *Issues in American Social Work*, pp. 242–269. New York: Columbia University Press.

Vollmer, Howard M. and Donald L. Mills, eds. 1966. *Professionalization*. Englewood Cliffs, NJ: Prentice-Hall.

Wagenaar, Theodore C. 1974. "Activist professionals: the case of teachers." *Social Science Quarterly* 55:372–379.

Wagner, David. 1987. "Political ideology and professional careers: a study of radical social service workers." Ph.D. dissertation, City University of New York.

Wagner, David, and Marcia B. Cohen. 1978. "Social workers' class, and professionalism." *Catalyst* 1:25–55.

Wallace, Marquis E. 1982. "Private practice: a nationwide study." *Social Work* 27:262–267.

Wallace, Marquis E. 1977. "Autonomy in private practice." Ph.D. dissertation, University of Chicago.

Walsh, James Leo, and Ray H. Elling. 1972. "Professionalism and the poor—structural effects and professional behavior." In Eliot Freidson and Judith Lorber, *Medical Men and Their Work*, pp. 267–283. Chicago: Aldine Atherton, Inc.

Ward, James, Jacque E. Gibbons, Henry J. Comp, and Marvin A. Kaiser. 1985. "Professionalism: does social work education make a difference?" *Arête* 10:15–25.

Weaver, Jerry L. 1981. "The elderly as a political community: the case of national health policy." In Robert B. Hudson, ed., *The Aging in Politics: Process and Policy*, pp. 30–42. Springfield, IL: Charles C. Thomas.

Weick, Ann. 1980. "Issues of power in social work practice." In Ann Weick and Susan T. Vandiver, eds., *Women, Power, and Change*, pp. 173–185. Washington, D.C.: National Association of Social Workers.

Weissman, Harold H., ed. 1969. *Community Development in the Mobilization for Youth Experience*. New York: Association Press.

Weissman, Harold H., ed. 1969. *Employment and Education Services in the Mobilization for Youth Experience*. New York: Association Press.

Weissman, Harold H., ed. 1969. *Individual and Group Services in the Mobilization for Youth Experience*. New York: Association Press.

Weissman, Harold H., ed. 1969. *Justice and the Law in the Mobilization for Youth Experience*. New York: Association Press.

Wilding, Paul. 1982. *Professional Power and Social Welfare*. London: Routledge and Kegan Paul.

Wilensky, Harold L. 1964. "The professionalization of everyone." *American Journal of Sociology* 70: 137–158.

Wilensky, Harold L., and Charles N. Lebeaux. 1965. *Industrial Society and Social Welfare*. 2d ed. New York: Macmillan Publishing Co., Inc., Free Press Paperback.

Wills, Garry. "New votuhs." (Review of Frances Fox Piven and Richard A. Cloward's book, *Why Americans Don't Vote*.) *The New York Review of Books*. August 18, 1988:3–5.

Wilson, G. 1976. "From practice to theory: a personalized history." In R. Roberts and H. Nathen, eds., *Theories of Social Work With Groups,* pp. 1–44. New York: Columbia University Press.

Wilson, Paul A., Victor Voth, and Walter W. Hudson. 1980. "Professionals and the bureaucracy: measuring the orientations of social workers." *Journal of Social Service Research* 4:15–30.

Woodroofe, Kathleen. 1962. *From Charity to Social Work.* London: Routledge and Kegan Paul.

Yohalem, Alice M. 1979. *The Careers of Professional Women: Commitment and Conflict.* Montclair, NJ: Allenheld Osmun and Co.

INDEX